SMOKEY

SMOKEY

The True Stories behind
the University of Tennessee's
Beloved Mascot

Thomas J. Mattingly

Earl C. Hudson

THE UNIVERSITY OF TENNESSEE PRESS / KNOXVILLE

Copyright © 2012 by The University of Tennessee Press / Knoxville.
All Rights Reserved. Manufactured in the United States of America.
First Edition.

The paper in this book meets the requirements of American National Standards Institute / National Information Standards Organization specification
Z39.48–1992 (Permanence of Paper). It contains 30 percent post-consumer
waste and is certified by the Forest Stewardship Council.

Library of Congress Cataloging-in-Publication Data

Mattingly, Thomas J.
Smokey: the true stories behind the University of Tennessee's beloved mascot /
Thomas J. Mattingly, Earl C. Hudson. — 1st ed.
        p. cm.
ISBN-13: 978-1-57233-917-0 (hardback)
ISBN-10: 1-57233-917-9 (hardcover)

    1. University of Tennessee, Knoxville—Football—History.
    2. Tennessee Volunteers (Football team)—History.
    3. Smokey (Dog)
    4. University of Tennessee, Knoxville—Mascots—History.
    5. School mascots—Tennessee—History.
    6. University of Tennessee, Knoxville—Sports—History.
    I. Hudson, Earl C.
    II. Title.

GV958.U586M38 2012
371.009768′85—dc23
                        2012028720

"America has always had a famous animal. With the exception of Secretariat and an animated mouse named Mickey, it's usually a dog. In years gone by, Rin Tin Tin was king of the canines, then Lassie."

—Sonny Seiler and Kent Hannon, *Damn Good Dogs*

"There is greatness in all dogs and all breeds. There is a quality about a blue tick coonhound that just puts a catch in your heart. It may be the incongruity of the breed—here is a dog with the endurance and fortitude to trail and track all night, the intelligence and instinct to follow a lead across miles of unfamiliar mountains, and the uncanny ability to turn up the next morning—with torn pads and ears—in the same spot where the hunt began, waiting stoically for his human to find him. Seemingly imperturbable with their doleful expressions and simple needs, they are also almost heartbreakingly vulnerable—as if their contentment with humble fare is a defense against the possibility that there may never be more offered. But nothing compares to the adoring look in those houndly eyes, nor the profound sigh of bliss when that large head is lowered onto your lap to receive gentle petting. Euphoric appreciation attends every meal placed before a coon hound, and there is not another dog we know who can appreciate with such utter abandon the exquisite comfort of a soft, fleecy bed."

—http://www.bluetickcoonhound.info/

CONTENTS

Acknowledgments   xiii

1. Prologue: The Magic of University of Tennessee Football   1

2. Looking Back: Smokey in Context   17

3. The 1953 University of Tennessee Campus Scene:
          A Much Kinder and Gentler Place   27

4. The Tide of Times in Tennessee Football, 1953:
          Never Follow a Legend   41

5. The Bluetick Cometh   51

6. The Legacy of the Smokeys   73

Epilogue: Final Thoughts on the Smokeys and a Look to the Future   103

Notes   111
Index   119

ILLUSTRATIONS

FIGURES

Smokey IX and AGR Handlers Run the Field   2

Program Featuring Smokey, 1978 Game in Memphis   3

Charlie Daniel Cartoon Featuring Smokey, Auburn Tiger,
          and the War Eagle, 1977   5

Alpha Gamma Rho House   7

Smokey's Bed at the AGR House   8

Smokey at the Center of Attention at Tailgate Parties on Game Days   9

Smokey IX in a Pensive Mood   11

Gavin McManusShows off a Smokey Backpack   12

Earl Hudson and Smokey VIII on the Back Porch   13

Rev. Bill Brooks and Smokey I with Security Contingent
          at Shields-Watkins Field   21

Sports Editor Tom Siler and General Robert Neyland   23

A L'il Abner motif on September 26, 1953, Featuring Smokey I   25

The Early 1950s Shields-Watkins Field   28

Science Hall, U.T. Campus   29

Wide Receiver Lester McClain   35

Albert Davis at Signing Ceremony   36

President Andy Holt   39

University of Tennessee's 1953 Football Schedule   42

General Neyland   43

Coach Harvey Robinson   44

Bowden Wyatt Talks with University of Tennessee Students   47

Coach Bowden Wyatt   48

Bill Brooks's Clutch Shop   52

An Early Shot of the Vol Network   54

Smokey III and a Tennessee Walking Horse   59

"Blue Smoky" and U.T. Cheerleaders   60

Bowden Wyatt with John Majors and "Papa" John Gordy   62

Jackie Parker, 1953 Mississippi State Star   65

Smokey I with an Early Handler   67

·Smokey I on a White Carpet, 1953 Duke Game   70

Smokey Being Weighed Somewhere on Campus, 1953   71

A Very Young Pup that Would Become Smokey II   74

Smokey III with Jeannie Gilbert and Keith Richardson   75

Smokey VII around 1992 or 1993   76

Smokey VIII Looking Happy   77

Smokey IX Relaxing in the Midst of His Hectic Schedule   78

Smokey I Was Killed on this Deserted Stretch of U.S. Highway 11W   79

Will Haynes's Consolation Letter   80

Postcard from Smokey's Dognappers   84

Charlie Daniel Tribute to General Neyland   89

Charlie Daniel Cartoon Celebrating 1968 Victory over Alabama   90

Majorette Becky Nanney with Smokey III   91

Smokey V and UGA Get to Know Each Other, 1980 Georgia Game   92

Smokey V Honored as One of the "Dogs of the SEC" in 1981   93

Bill and Mildred Brooks in the 1980s   94

Closeup of Smokey VIII   96

Smokey IX Takes a Snooze   98

Russ Goes Nose-to-Nose with Smokey IX   99

Smokey IX Takes a Sniff at the "Human Smokey"   101

Primary and Secondary Marks, University of Tennessee   105

Earl and Martha with Smokey VIII   107

Smokey IX at Charles Hudson's House   108

Beware of the Dog   110

PLATES

Following Page   72

Smokey I

Smokey II

Smokey III

Smokey IV

Smokey V

Smokey VI

Smokey VII

Smokey VIII

Smokey IX

ACKNOWLEDGMENTS

Assembling a book such as this one is no easy task, especially when the subject matter goes back some sixty years. A number of people have helped greatly along the way. The destination has certainly been worth the journey.

This is a story that has a definite beginning—the University of Tennessee Pep Club contest to choose a mascot in 1953. Nearly sixty years later, the story of the mascot is still evolving, with the ninth version of a Bluetick Coonhound contributing to the history.

There wouldn't be a history of the Smokeys without the Brooks and Hudson families of Knoxville. Bill and Mildred Brooks made a promise to Stuart Worden in 1953 that there would be a dog available for every game, and the families have kept that promise. Earl and Martha Hudson picked up the torch and kept the commitment alive. Earl's son, Charles, now has Smokey IX in his care. It's a family story from the word go.

Students from the early 1950s, such as Stuart Worden, Wawanna Cameron Widoff, Harvey Sproul, Rev. Gordon Goodgame, and Hal Ernest answered every question patiently and thoroughly throughout the writing process. Stuart's son, John, was likewise helpful, providing scans of the 1953 festivities at Shields-Watkins Field. Their interviews appear throughout the text, and I have chosen, in the interest of readability, not to make formal references to them each and every time their words appear.

Smokey IX's 2011–12 handler, Robert Moser, provided perspective on life with the Bluetick, sitting patiently for an interview the day before he and Smokey IX left for the 2011 Alabama–Tennessee football game in Tuscaloosa. His fellow handler, James Berlin (Trey) McAdams III now in charge in 2012–13, led a tour of the Alpha Gamma Rho house on campus and provided his thoughts on Smokey IX and the entire tradition of the dogs relative to the AGR fraternity.

Elsewhere in the university, there was considerable assistance from the Special Collections staff at the Hodges Library, the Microfilm Archives (located in three different locations during the preparation of this book, most recently at the Hoskins Library), and the University's Center for Video and Photography in the Student Services Building. They have always been exceptionally helpful, occasionally finding stuff we weren't sure existed.

From the University of Tennessee Press, Scot Danforth provided capable counsel and occasionally added a well-turned phrase. Tom Post likewise provided inspiration, as did Thomas Wells.

Bill Dye was a *Knoxville News Sentinel* photographer who was right in the middle of the kidnapping of Smokey II by students at the University of Kentucky, along with colleague Mickey Creager. Before his death in the summer of 2009, Bill shared his perspective on the way the "dognapping story" developed. His son, Rick, helped fill in the gaps and added his unique perspective on Bill's career with the *News Sentinel*.

Haywood Harris, Bill Dyer, Dr. Andy Kozar, and Lindsey Nelson, each now deceased, were likewise influential on the author's writing career. Kozar was a "historian's historian," while Haywood and Lindsey chronicled the history of the Vol football program in their writings, and Bill drew a cartoon version of Tennessee games from 1934 to his death in late October 1976. We miss all of them in the Knoxville sports community.

Marvin West, former sports editor of the *Knoxville News Sentinel*, has been a significant mentor over the years and helped out when words wouldn't pass through the fingers onto the keyboard to the computer screen.

Bud Ford, John Painter, Susie Treis, Jimmy Stanton, and Jason Yellin opened up the files and archives of the University of Tennessee Sports Information Office, helping with pictures, game programs, picture scans, and magazine articles relative to the Bluetick Coonhound. Steve Early of the Vol Network helped find various tapes and other Tennessee football information, as did Jeff Jacoby of Knoxville radio station WNML, who has a unique ability to cite famous John Ward calls over the years . . . from memory.

Joy Postell-Gee did likewise with Spirit Office.

Matt Dixon, 2011–12 sports editor of the *Daily Beacon*, located any number of pictures and captions from the U.T. Photographic Services, just around the corner from his office in the Communications Building.

Knoxville News Sentinel staff members, led by editor Jack McElroy, executive sports editor Phil Kaplan, columnist Sam Venable, and cartoonist Charlie Daniel, were extremely supportive of the project from the beginning, offering all types of helpful advice.

Don Carringer of *Football Time in Tennessee* provided pictures of the more recent Smokeys, as did Jack Williams, recently retired from the University of Tennessee's President's Office, a multi-talented man who can always deliver whatever you need exactly when you need it.

The Mattingly family—my wife, Susan, son, Sam, daughter, Alice, and her husband, Brad McManus—were always patient and helpful during the manuscript preparation process. Gavin Stewart McManus came along in August 2010 to brighten all of our lives further.

1

PROLOGUE: THE MAGIC OF UNIVERSITY OF TENNESSEE FOOTBALL

"Tennessee fans here and throughout the country listening to this broadcast have begun to experience the feeling of excitement as the University of Tennessee Pride of the Southland Marching Band marches from the formation facing the south end zone, where the national anthem has just been played and sung, into the traditional T stretching from the east stands, the corridor leading from the Vol dressing room to the west sidelines. The band is there . . . there are thousands of balloons as well. And now, as Tennessee comes onto the field, 'It's Football Time in Tennessee.' College football at its finest . . . 60 seconds for our stations as we say, 'This is the Vol Network. Get ready for the kickoff.'"

—John Ward, the "Voice of the Vols,"
Tennessee–Alabama game, October 16, 1982

And a hound shall lead them.

Not any "hound," mind you, but a Bluetick Coonhound named Smokey, a breed native to the state of Tennessee.[1]

When the Tennessee Volunteers football team is massed at the north end of Shields-Watkins Field, ready to take on all comers in front of more than 100,000 fans, the Pride of the Southland Marching Band prepares to open the

There's nothing like that magic moment when Smokey, accompanied by his AGR handlers, leads the Vols onto Shields-Watkins Field just before kickoff. From Earl Hudson scrapbook.

giant "T," stretching southward down the greensward, it's a great moment for Tennessee fans, one of the great moments in all of college football.

As the crowd noise swells, the band plays the "Spirit of the Hill," forming the "T." When the "T" opens and the strains of "Down the Field" echo across Neyland Stadium, the Bluetick, accompanied by his two handlers from the Alpha Gamma Rho (AGR) fraternity—they refer to their thirty-five year experience with Smokey as one of their finest achievements—has traditionally been the first one through, howling loudly as he makes his entrance.[2]

When the *Knoxville News Sentinel* wanted to hype the University of Tennessee Library's efforts to digitize Tennessee football game programs in an article published on November 2, 2011, to whom did they turn to as an example of what fans might find in those volumes?

The Bluetick Coonhounds named Smokey, that's who: all nine of them.

"Fans can read about thrilling victories and crushing defeats, influential coaches and players. They also can reminisce about UT rivalries, retired Vol

Smokey has often been a part of the cover art for Tennessee football game programs. This one shows Smokey and the Mississippi State Bulldog clashing before the 1978 game in Memphis. The artist is D. C. Moody, a graphic designer from Oswego, Kansas. U.T. Sports Information Office.

jerseys, and Smokey's lineage and adventures. (For example: Did you know Smokey II survived both a dognapping and a confrontation with the Baylor Bear?)"[3]

Charles Daniel, a well-known Knoxville editorial cartoonist who has drawn for both the *Knoxville Journal* and the *Knoxville News Sentinel* during his long career, was impressed enough with Smokey's tenure and the overall ambience of his presence on Shields-Watkins Field that he devoted a whole book of his cartoons to the dog and the team. This book is called *UT Football Cartoons by Daniel, with Some Free Thoughts by Ben Byrd,* one of four books of cartoons he's assembled over the course of his career.

Throughout the book, Daniel draws the Smokey mascot in various scenarios, depending on the game. The dog is often shown without identification, sometimes captioned with the name "Smokey," and captioned more generically with "UT."[4] Smokey also makes cameo appearances in Daniel's other books.[5] Daniel once lovingly termed Smokey the "Orange Nose Hound Dog."

Smokey appears constantly in the front-page cartoons in each Knoxville newspaper on game days and on the editorial pages of the daily newspapers. While Smokey has achieved near-mythical status in the local media, symbolically linked to all the fortunes (and misfortunes) of U.T.'s athletic teams, he is as real a Bluetick as you'll ever find.

"For pure pageantry and showmanship, the Pride of the Southland Band is hard to beat," Ron Smith, author of *Every Saturday in Autumn: College Football's Greatest Traditions,* argues. "But Smokey, the blue tick coon hound that serves as Tennessee's mascot, is No. 1 in the hearts of Volunteer fans."[6]

In a day in which tradition is something happening yesterday, not being given the respect and reverence it deserves, the continuing presence of a Bluetick Coonhound for sixty years as the University of Tennessee's first (and only) mascot speaks for itself. But where did these familiar notions about mascots come from? It's a fascinating story in its own right.

"The tradition of mascots in the United States goes back at least as far as the Civil War where many regiments had living mascots," Adriana Norton writes, noting that "In the post Civil War era, intercollegiate and interschool competition began using mascots when intercollegiate athletic games and rivalries emerged." She also points out that "Some schools do not have mascots, Michigan being a notable example. Its athletic department has maintained there was no need of one and that one would not reflect the spirit and values of athletics at the university. It has refused to sanction one even though over

September 24, 1977   Auburn 14   Vols 12

Knoxville Journal cartoonist Charlie Daniel shows a growling Smokey getting acquainted with the Auburn Tiger and the "War Eagle, September 24, 1977." Courtesy *Knoxville News Sentinel*.

the years, mascots in a variety of wolverine costumes have been proposed." Then from the perspective of history, she writes, "The word mascot came into the English language from a French word used to describe anything which brought luck to a household."[7]

For the fans, mascots are part of keeping tradition alive, helping pass the torch from generation to generation. Devoted football fans, particularly in the South, make critical, life-changing decisions about team allegiance in their most tender years and live with the impact of those decisions throughout the rest of their lives. There seem to be precious few times these allegiances change.

"As alumni," ESPN analyst Kirk Herbstreit observes, "you have a love affair with the team because that's your place. Students know that their parents and grandparents went to school there and experienced many of the same things. Now it's their turn. It's their first chance to experience all the things they've been told about."[8] A *Yahoo* sports story from November 2, 2011, contends that "Students remember their alma mater's traditions long after they've forgotten much of what they learned in a classroom."[9]

To say there's been a love affair between Tennessee fans and each of the Smokeys would be an understatement. The dog is an integral part of the game-day experience.

SMOKEY ON GAME DAY

Most people will tell you that having a dog around the house has always been an adventure. Earl Hudson knows that as well as anybody, having had Smokey VII, Smokey VIII, and Smokey IX as part of his home life on Mountaincrest Drive. So do the brothers at the Alpha Gamma Rho fraternity house on the Tennessee campus.

Smokey IX enjoys the surroundings in Earl's yard, sunning himself in the backyard and occasionally slipping through the fence to visit a neighbor's front porch. Earl's home is located on an isolated end of a short street, one not burdened by a great deal of traffic. It's in distinct contrast to Rev. Bill Brooks's home on Rutledge Pike, a major thoroughfare of the 1950s, where Smokey I was killed by an oncoming motorist.

Smokey's doleful bark is a part of the quiet neighborhood's ambience. The one-word description, Earl Hudson said, of Smokey's voice wafting through the neighborhood is "melodious."

But there was more to being the mascot of the Tennessee Volunteers than the good life in Earl's back yard. Smokey IX makes a great many public appearances during the football season and attends games, home and away, with his handlers from the Alpha Gamma Rho (AGR) fraternity.

"He's definitely a homebody," Earl Hudson says. "But when it's time for the handlers to pick him up, he's definitely ready. I'll dress him, and he'll wait in the living room for them to arrive. He has a sixth sense about when they'll get to the house." Earl says that Smokey leaves the house on Friday afternoon and returns home by the middle of Sunday afternoon, no worse for the wear and tear of a game at Neyland Stadium or wherever else the Vols might play.

So, as game day approaches, it's off to his second home. When Smokey IX is on campus before or after a game, you can find him in Room 203 of the Alpha Gamma Rho house on Fraternity Row. It's a typical collegiate dorm room, with all the accoutrements of campus life, a trifle messy, perhaps, but Smokey IX is just glad to be a part of the team, just glad to have a soft bed after his day's work.

It's a dog's life, in the best sense of that term. He sleeps on a small bed, always accompanied by a tattered orange blanket. Would Smokey IX want any other color? "His orange blanket is his pride and joy. He won't sleep without it," said 2012–13 handler James Berlin (Trey) McAdams III, a senior in marketing from Brownsville, Tennessee. "He's definitely the 'King of the House' when he's here. He's well behaved most of the time, but he can get a little cranky."

The Alpha Gamma Rho House on campus. Tom Mattingly.

The pooch is much in demand for public appearances throughout the year, but especially during game week. Hardly a week goes by that he's not making an appearance somewhere.

A typical home game-day itinerary, 2011–12 handler Robert Moser says, might include a visit to Vol Village, a pregame gathering place for students and fans, and Circle Park, a central location that teems with fans on game day. In addition, Smokey might be accompanied for a jaunt down Peyton Manning Pass for the Vol Walk, when players and coaches enter the stadium a couple of hours before the game begins, and a visit to the Chancellor's tailgate. That's in addition to the game. That also doesn't include the adulation Smokey IX receives on his way to and from each of these events.

On Homecoming Day, there might be even more stops, what with class reunions and other events on campus. Smokey IX can't sneak in anywhere. He's a recognizable figure on campus to young and old alike.

"No one really knows how many fans have had their picture taken with any of the Smokeys," Earl Hudson said, estimating only that it's been "a bunch." Moser calls his association with Smokey IX a "life-altering experience" and tells what those final, frantic moments with the dog were like as the team prepares to come through the "T."

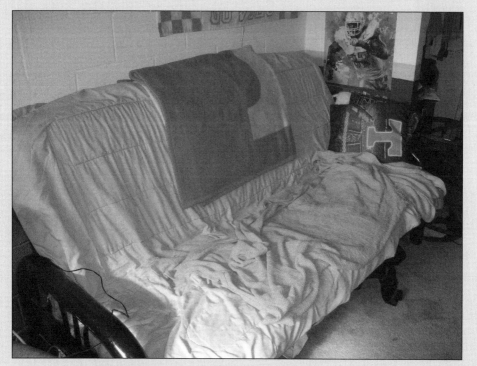

Smokey IX's bed at the AGR house. The blanket is orange, of course. Tom Mattingly.

"We start walking down the east sidelines after the 'National Anthem,'" Moser said in October 2011. "Once we get to the north end under the goal post (we don't go all the way into the tunnel), there's no holding him back. He wants to go. He's woofing the whole time. When the 'T' opens, he has his head down, running as fast as he can."

At that point, it's not clear who has control of whom, but, regardless, it's still a marvelous sight, part of college football's finest pre-game show. "It's a big responsibility," Moser said. "It's made me more responsible."

What is Smokey IX's take on the excitement leading the team onto the field? A November 2005 *Southern Living* "interview" with Smokey IX gives his "answer": "Man, that's another rush. . . . More than 108,000 fans are cheering! What a moment! Chasing squirrels dims in comparison."

After leading the Vols through the "T," Smokey IX finds his place on the east side, south end, with the cheerleaders and his handlers. He might sneak a nap here and there, but he appears to be eternally vigilant. The television cameras keep a close

Smokey always seems to be the center of attention at tailgates across the campus on game days.

watch on him, and it's not uncommon to see a woofing Smokey as part of the intro-
ductory package that leads into the telecast of a Tennessee game.

To say there's been a love affair between Tennessee fans and each of the
Smokeys would be an understatement. The dog is an integral part of the game
day experience. "This is the aspect of fraternity life we take the most pride in,"
McAdams says.

The line of Smokeys outstrips even the more famous Uga, the Georgia
Bulldogs' line of mascots, in terms of service. Uga made his first appearance
in Athens in 1956, a few years after Smokey appeared in Knoxville. They're as
different as two dogs could be, yet each of them is revered by their respective
fan base.

A 2004 *Sports Illustrated* article paints a vivid picture of the game-day experience at a U.T. home game:

> Think your school's game-day experience is all that and a bag of chips? Universities like to carry the one definitive aspect of their programs around like a trump card. But Tennessee sees whatever your school is bringing to the table and bets the House That General Neyland Built that it's got you beat. Tennessee has it all. What's the competition holding? Washington shows its floating tailgate off Puget Sound only to have Tennessee match it with the Volunteer Navy. Next up is Georgia and its famous bulldog, Uga. Sorry. Compared with Smokey, Tennessee's unflappable bluetick coonhound, Uga looks as clichéd as a poker-playing bulldog. Michigan and Ohio State put up the Big House (2003 average attendance: 110,918) and the pregame dotting of the i, respectively. Tennessee, however, responds with its own six-digit crowds ('03 average: 105,038), which detonate as the Vols run through the fabled T before the game. The challengers keep coming: Auburn's Tiger Walk, Nebraska's Sea of Red and West Virginia's Country Roads. Tennessee answers: Vol Walk, Orange Nation, Rocky Top. And don't forget the fabled checkerboard end zone. King the Vols.

Smokey IX stands 24 inches high and weighs 64 pounds and helps reflect the tradition and heritage of a great university from across the years. The Bluetick Coonhound is a constant reminder of university life at Tennessee, reflecting what the university means to its alumni.

That's what mascots, often considered to be the face of their universities, do.

Over the years, the name Smokey has resounded across campus and wherever Vol fans might gather. There was *Smokey's Tale,* an official publication of the Athletic Department. There was Smokey's Howl, a campus pep rally and gathering point on game days. There was a student eatery called Smokey's Palace in the Carolyn P. Brown Student Center on campus. On the utsports.com website, there are any number of entries for Smokey "stuff," including playing cards, hats, dolls, collectible figurines, backpacks, sweatshirts, and t-shirts of all descriptions. There are also all types of Smokey items at the U.T. Student Center, Knoxville-area Cracker Barrel restaurants, and anywhere else prod-

Smokey IX in a pensive mood along the Tennessee sidelines. Photo courtesy Jack Williams.

ucts associated with the University of Tennessee are on sale. Smokey's mug even appears on a game called "Volopoly."

Smokey has adorned and been analyzed somewhat in many books. Smokey III, described as a "spirited blue tick coon hound," appeared along with head coach Doug Dickey, quarterback Bubba Wyche, and All-Americans Richmond Flowers, Steve Kiner, and Jack "Hacksaw" Reynolds in a 1983 book entitled *Football Powers of the South*. Smokey VIII appeared on the front and back

Gavin McManus, grandson of author Tom Mattingly, shows off a Smokey backpack from Christmas 2011. Photo courtesy Heather Lynch.

cover of a book entitled *Neyland: Life of a Stadium,* written by Barry Parker and Robin Hood.

Smokey IX appeared on the frontispiece of *The University of Tennessee All-Access Football Vault.* Smokey has also been featured in two fun children's books.[10]

Smokeys VIII and IX appeared in a special Tennessee section of *Southern Living* in November 2005. "No other school has a cheer quite like it," the article written by Gary D. Ford begins. "When Smokey howls, Volunteer fans leap to their feet and howl right back." In the October 2006 issue of *Southern Living,* Smokey IX earned mention in "40 reasons to Love Tennessee," the pooch being described and pictured as the "Tennessee Vols' biggest fan."

Author Earl Hudson and Smokey VIII on the back porch of Earl's home on Mountaincrest Drive in North Knoxville. Earl Hudson collection.

Smokey IX even appeared on Animal Planet's *Dogs 101* show in October 2011, with footage shot from Tennessee football games and from Earl Hudson's home and kennel.

Smokey IX's name was also brought into the debate over expansion in the Southeastern Conference. An anonymous e-mail informs Texas A&M and Missouri about what they could expect once they started competing in the conference. "Some teams in the SEC have more than one mascot, though they will tell you that they do not. The Tennessee Volunteers are represented by a dog, and I have never made the connection between the two. Auburn will tell you that they are the Tigers, and 'War Eagle' is only their battle cry—except that they have an eagle at all of their home games. The Alabama Crimson

Tide's mascot is Bear Bryant's ghost and an elephant, which is notably not a tide of any sort. And Ole Miss is a case study in multiple personality disorder that we will get to shortly."

After reading Richard Ernsberger Jr.'s book *Bragging Rights: A Season Inside the SEC, College Football's Toughest Conference,* it was disappointing to see that Smokey, for all his charm from the get-go, not to mention his longevity, did not make Ernsberger's list as the SEC's best mascot. The author, whose father, Dick, played fullback at Tennessee in the pre-Smokey days from 1949 to 1951, argues that Uga is the best and LSU's tiger, named Mike, is number 2. He might reconsider in the second edition, if there is one.[11]

Nevertheless, Smokey has a huge presence on campus and across Big Orange Country, but why should we care, at all, about the history of the nine Smokeys, from the initial selection to the evolution of the mascot over the years? A book entitled *Saturday Shrines: College Football's Most Hallowed Grounds* contains part of the answer. "General Robert Neyland, the SEC and national titles, the checkerboard end zones, the smoke off the mountains, they're all part of the lore of Tennessee football. And how about being named after the thousands of volunteers Gen. Andrew Jackson corralled and led to battle in the War of 1812? Thus the name Volunteers—or Vols. That's history. So is Smokey, the famed blue tick coon hound who leads the Vols through the 'T' at the beginning of the game and stays on the sideline as inspiration."[12]

As the years have passed, there have been a number of stories told about Smokey, many apocryphal, many anecdotal, many just plain wrong. There's no perspective on the dog's entire history. That's unfortunate, because the line of Smokeys has literally stood the test of time. It's an inspiring story, a story reflecting love of school, commitment to a person's word, and all those other eternal values we hold so dear in our society, sometimes more in the breach than in the observance. The historian's job, therefore, is to try to "get it right," to explain how and why the mascot was chosen, how he fits into the history of a great university.

Knoxvillian Bill Landry, former host of regional WBIR television's *Heartland Series,* argues, "Everything has to be written down, doesn't it? Stories. Tales. TV shows. It kind of makes it final and real."[13]

To make it "final and real" where the line of Smokeys is concerned, I had to make a decision. After all, in a professional career spanning more than thirty-five years, writing on any number of subjects ranging from energy issues to sports to politics and all points in between, I had never prepared a biography, a profile, even, of a subject who couldn't talk back (though, truth be told, there were a few human subjects who *wouldn't* talk back), one who literally couldn't sit still for an interview, one who walked on four legs.

But, in the case of the long line of dogs named Smokey, I decided to make an exception. After all, I had access to a number of interviews with Reverend W. C. Brooks, Smokey's original owner from nearly sixty years ago, as well as with co-author Earl C. Hudson, who has, until late 2011, had Smokey IX living at his home in a pleasant suburban neighborhood in north Knoxville.

There were still students from the era of Smokey's origins, such as Stuart Worden, Harvey Sproul, Rev. Gordon Goodgame, Hal Ernest, Wawanna Cameron Widoff, and others, who very well remember what all the fuss was about.

For their part, Tennessee fans have seen at least one, maybe more, maybe all of the nine Smokeys who have graced the sidelines at a Tennessee football game. The Smokeys are part of the extended family of Tennessee athletics.

Smokey's story does involve a great many people, people whose lives have revolved around a Bluetick Coonhound . . . and the University of Tennessee.

It's the same today.

"It's football time in Tennessee and a you can't play Tennessee ball without Smokey the Blue Tick Hound," Tom Poste wrote. "Coaches, players and athletic directors come and go, but Smokey is forever. The fans may turn on the players and run coaches and [athletic directors] out on a rail, but Smokey is top dog, year after year."[14]

This, then, is the story, the continuing legend of the Smokeys and their influence on a great university.

2

LOOKING BACK:
SMOKEY IN CONTEXT

When a caller knocked on Earl Hudson's front door at his home on Mountaincrest Drive in a pleasant section of North Knoxville suburbia, ignoring the posted sign reading "Beware of the Dog," there are two things you could count on.

First of all, you would be as welcome a houseguest as anybody could imagine, thanks to Earl's first wife, Martha, who died on November 29, 2005, or his second spouse, the former Bernice Burchett, who became Mrs. Hudson on April 26, 2008.

Secondly, a Bluetick Coonhound would come quickly, howling vociferously, and greeting the visitor with two large paws, a wet tongue, and a nose. If the dog isn't in the house, he's lounging in the back yard, his plaintive wail echoing across the neighborhood.

This is not just any dog, mind you, but Smokey IX, the mascot of the University of Tennessee Volunteers, and the most recent in a series of dogs that has engendered great emotion, love, and loyalty from Vol fans.

To his credit, Smokey has given back the love and attention to his fans.

"In these gentle giants' demeanor there are recognition and abject gratitude for the love they inspire in a human heart," an anonymous expert on Blueticks wrote in a spotlight feature on the petfinder.org website.

"Coonhounds bond in a deep and undemanding manner. Their easy-going personalities help them settle into the rhythms of home life easily and naturally, and they are perfect examples of how to make the most of any situation—

from down time to play time—no dog sleeps better, bounds into the car more joyously, endures more patiently, or loves more faithfully than a Bluetick Coonhound."[1]

Over the years, Smokey has expanded his household to the hearts of fans all across the expanse of Big Orange Country.

If Earl's neighbors are upset with having the Tennessee mascot within earshot, no one says anything.

"The neighbors don't mind," Earl said. "He doesn't howl much. We bring him in at night. He sleeps downstairs and sleeps through the night.

"He's scared of lighting and thunder. Their perception is greater than ours. They can sense thunder miles away. He doesn't tolerate loud noise and hides under the bed."

It might seem outlandish, but that's the beauty of it all.

Earl Hudson said in 2004 that the University of Tennessee wanted a dog "that would howl, and whose voice would carry and fire up the team."

A mascot is an animal or a thing believed to bring good luck—a sacred symbol of a particular group, especially of a sports team. But there's also a contrasting idea among certain fans, the grumps who worry that the sky might be falling every time a team loses or struggles, that a collegiate mascot is nothing special, really, nothing worth getting excited about. Mascots might be fun to watch, but are nothing of real importance.

Through the years, especially at the outset, some otherwise rational people have thought this was way too much fuss over a "mere" dog, even in Big Orange country.

"Why a football mascot at all?" *Knoxville News Sentinel* sports editor Tom Siler wondered in a February 4, 1955, article, shortly after Smokey I was struck and killed in front of Reverend Brooks's home by an unknown motorist. "After all, the Volunteers had done pretty well, 1926–52, without a mascot."

Siler, a two-time president of the U.T. Alumni Association, was one of those in the community who favored the Tennessee Walking Horse as a mascot, if there were to be one. At the time, Siler also worried—needlessly, it seems—that Bluetick Coonhounds did not have the "dash and spirit and fire that characterizes college football." He thought, as a result of having a hound as a mascot, outsiders might perceive that U.T. was a "hillbilly school," a term "often used contemptuously."

Smokey has a way of winning over the doubters, and Siler was no exception. He did recant and acknowledged the hound's impact in a 1970 book, writing in part, "Football has become a label, a tag, a brand name, if you please . . . It means Smoky, the blue tick hound mascot, beloved of the 22,000 students."[2]

In general, those who downplay the role of mascots miss out on one of the great thrills in the pageantry of college football. Although the line of Smokeys has been around a long time, the mascot grew out of a context of these symbols from universities around the country.

"At the college level alone," according to a 2005 USAToday.com story entitled, "The top mascots in college and professional sports," there are "more than 1,700 mascots and nicknames from which to select." The collegiate mascots, big or small, are beloved within every university community. And that's putting it mildly. Some of them are pretty exotic. LSU has Mike the Tiger, Texas has a Longhorn steer named Bevo, Colorado has an American Bison named Ralphie, USC a horse named Traveler, and so on.[3]

Among colleges and universities, dogs are represented more than their fair share. Other than Uga, there is Ben, the English Bulldog mascot of McPherson College, Handsome Dan, the Bulldog mascot at Yale, Jack, the English Bulldog mascot of the Georgetown Hoyas, King Husky of Northeastern University, Lulu, the female Bulldog mascot and Mac T. Bulldog, the male mascot of Gardner-Webb, Reveille, the collie at Texas A&M, Rhett, the Boston Terrier mascot at Boston University, the Saluki dog from Southern Illinois, Scottie, the mascot at Agnes Scott, Spike from Gonzaga and Samford, and Timeout, the costumed Bulldog at Fresno State.

Out of all the mascot names and breeds listed, there is only one Bluetick Coonhound mascot, and that hound is named Smokey.

Where Smokey's selection in September 1953 is concerned, however, the historians just didn't get it wrong. They just didn't get it.

In September 1953, a group of University of Tennessee students (most of them now in their mid-to-late seventies), members of the school's Pep Club, made their mark on school history by sponsoring a contest to bring a mascot to campus in order to increase "school spirit" in those long-ago days. They probably didn't know it, but this would become a defining moment in their collegiate lives.

In any number of University of Tennessee histories and U.T.-related books, there is precious little discussion or analysis of the way the original Smokey, known then as "Brooks' Blue Smokey," was selected, beyond these "basic facts," the "cover story," if you will, as found in the 2010 *Tennessee Football Media Guide*.

The Tennessee students voted to select a live coonhound mascot to represent the school in 1953. The late Reverend Bill Brooks entered his prize-winning Bluetick Coonhound, "Brooks' Blue Smokey," in the selection contest. At halftime of the Mississippi State game that season, the dogs were introduced over the loudspeaker and the student body cheered for their favorite, with "Blue Smokey" responding to the fans with a bark of his own to secure the victory. The Smokey lineage—nine dogs in all—has stayed under the care of either Reverend Brooks' or his wife's family ever since. Smokey IX has been serving since the 2004 season.

Much about the early years is shrouded in myth and mystery, starting with the dog's name. Earl Hudson, Bill Brooks' brother-in-law and Smokey's keeper since 1994, recently observed that Bill likely chose the spelling "Smokey" to differentiate his dog from the spelling of the Great Smoky Mountains, the spectacular mountain range and national park that spans East Tennessee and Western North Carolina. Early local newspaper accounts from the *Knoxville Journal* and *Knoxville News Sentinel* often spelled the dog's name "Smoky"— at times in the early years, to many a proofreader's shame, both spellings appeared in the same story. In early 2012, Earl Hudson indicated that in those early days, "We might not have done a good job explaining the name."

Reverend Brooks, the original owner of Smokey and native of Rogersville, Tennessee, was as colorful an East Tennessean as you could find. He loved his family, the Baptist Church, the Bluetick Coonhound, and the Knoxville Volunteer Rescue Squad, an organization he founded ("along with Costo McGee," Earl said), more than likely in that order. For him, the hounds were always something special.

When Earl and Martha Hudson took over after Reverend Brooks and his wife, Mildred, had died, the family atmosphere continued. Earl's second wife, Bernice, who has admitted to not being a big dog lover, has since come around and become one of Smokey IX's strongest supporters and admirers.

"When he was on *Animal Planet,* he was the most beautiful dog there," Bernice said.

Over the years, the Smokeys have been a part of the great moments in Tennessee football history, standing eternally vigilant on the east sidelines of Shields-Watkins Field in front of the Tennessee student section.

Rev. Bill Brooks and Smokey I with security contingent at Shields-Watkins Field. This undated photo came from the Earl Hudson scrapbook. The caption read as follows: "Smoky, the Vols' mascot, came to the game with a police escort when rumors circulated that Kentucky football fans were planning to 'dognap' Smoky in reprisal for the recent 'kegnapping' at Lexington. The 'dognapping' failed to materialize. Shown with Smoky are his handler W. C. Brooks, center, and patrolmen Neal Long Jr. (left) and Bill Boyd, two of the biggest men on the force."

They've also been fixtures at games on the road—with a couple of exceptions. Smokey II was denied entrance to Grant Field in Atlanta in 1962 due to a local quarantine. He spent the game hours in a car with Mildred. Spirit coordinator Joy Postell-Gee also points out that Smokey has not been allowed recently into stadiums at Arkansas and Vanderbilt, since neither stadium now allows live animals inside the gates. (Arkansas does have its Razorback mascot inside the stadium, albeit in a cage. Smokey IX probably wouldn't do well in a cage.)

The Bluetick is much in demand for public appearances throughout the year, but especially during game week. Hardly a week goes by that he's not making an appearance somewhere.

The selection of a mascot, a rallying point for the Vol football program, in particular, and all its athletic teams, in general, was and remains a big deal.

Former University of Tennessee historian Dr. Milton Klein placed the process of selecting a mascot in context among the top historical events on campus, decisions that have shaped the university. Klein published a 1994 monograph, later updated in 1996, entitled *Volunteer Moments*. "We are fortunate in having several such memoirs of University of Tennessee students, presented in the vignettes below. They reveal the limited range of campus activities available under the male, military regime that prevailed until 1890, the changes that came with admission of women in 1892, the initiation of Homecoming, Torch Night, Aloha Oe ceremonies, and other ceremonies in the early twentieth century, and the adoption in recent years of a new team mascot, Smokey, the blue tick hound."[4]

Neal O'Steen of the University of Tennessee's Public Relations Office accurately wrote in 1980 that the selection of a mascot—a "natural," as he termed it—was part of a movement "calculated to lure fans to the games." O'Steen mentioned the new mascot, the newly-designated "Pride of the Southland Marching Band," and the "card section," with the student section spelling out messages and designs with multi colored cards as being important elements in creating a very popular, contemporary football program at U.T.[5]

It has now been nearly 60 years since a Smokey first took the field. Consider how long that's been.

All this fuss over a mascot happened before former Vol quarterback and 1974 co-captain Condredge Holloway was born (January 25, 1954), before there was a student center on campus, before 1952 Vol captain Jim Haslam founded Pilot Oil in 1958 as a single, family-owned gas station in Gate City, Virginia.

In those days, former University of Tennessee head football coach Doug Dickey and former Georgia head coach Vince Dooley were playing college football at Florida and Auburn, respectively. Former Vol head coach Bill Battle was nearly twelve years old, living in Birmingham, Alabama. Gen. Dwight David Eisenhower was nearly ten months into his first term as President of the United States.

In Knoxville, another general, the legendary Brig. Gen. Robert Reese Neyland, had just stepped down after a legendary career as Tennessee head coach, initially holding out the possibility he might come back to the Shields-

Watkins Field sidelines. Knoxville media and the 1953 *University of Tennessee Football Media Guide* each reported that he was "on leave of absence for a year because of ill health."

In a book entitled *Neyland: The Gridiron General,* Bob Gilbert wrote that General Neyland "requested a leave of absence for the 1953 season," a move supported by University President Dr. C. E. Brehm and the institution's Board of Trustees. "I have a definite understanding with the athletics board and trustees that when I get ready to quit active coaching, I will stay on here as athletic director during the remainder of my career," Neyland said.[6]

General Neyland never did return to coaching, but did continue to serve as director of athletics until his death in 1962.

It was, by any measure, a far different time.

Knoxville News Sentinel Sports Editor Tom Siler and General Bob Neyland watching a 1953 practice. *Knoxville News Sentinel.*

The 1953–54 *Volunteer* yearbook, edited by Barbara J. Moore, gives a sense of what the campus was like during that year.

In that volume, there is an artist's rendering of the "Student Activities Building," soon to become the University Center, later renamed the Carolyn P. Brown Memorial Student Center.

There was a dedicatory statement to Dean of Women Gladys Beach, saying, in part, "she is never too busy to listen to a little freshman tell of her scholastic difficulties, or help an upset transfer with her adjustments, or hear out an upperclassman having trouble with her love life."

Students, whether in fraternities or sororities or not, were pictured in row after row of thumbnails, all earnest looking in coats and ties for the men or dresses that were likely worn on church Sundays for the women.

The students were all white, and their hairstyles reflected the trends of the day.

Fraternity and sorority activities occurred at houses, most now demolished in the rush to modernize the campus, well before "Fraternity Row" on Volunteer Boulevard was even considered.

The editors of the 1953–54 *Volunteer* yearbook were obviously not impressed with the impact the selection of a mascot might have on the university community, not seeing things the way Dr. Klein did more than three decades later.

There was a page in the yearbook picturing Pep Club members, but no mention anywhere of the dog, and no pictures of him. There was a picture of a large paper cutout of Smokey I on a Pi Kappa Alpha fraternity Homecoming float before the LSU game on November 7.

Here's what the 1953–54 annual said about the Pep Club: "The Pep Club has taken a very active role in promoting spirit on 'the Hill.' During football season, the club held a 'bunny hop,' pajama parade, and pep rallies. They also chartered a bus to go to the Kentucky game last fall. During the winter quarter the club sponsored a 'King of Ugliness' contest as well as initiating 'sock hop' dances after the basketball games."

Pep Club president Stuart Worden did not know why the yearbook failed to report details about the contest to select the dog, but he thought it might have been an issue of timing—it could have been the yearbook had a tight printing deadline to meet. He did say the mascot selection process was a "very important step forward, as we tried to get more spirit around the games."

By the next year, the blackout began to lift, though slowly. The first pictures of Smokey I appear, uncaptioned, in the 1954–55 *Volunteer*. That volume does acknowledge the Pep Club's role in the Smokey saga, with the copy reading, in part: "The Pep Club is the backbone of spirit on the Hill. Throughout the year, the club is active in promoting pep rallies and parades, the sale of orange and white shakers and decorations, and half-time skits at football games. The club also sponsors the Best Yell Contest, trips to the out-of-town football and basketball games, and also many other activities. Smoky, the Volunteer mascot, was obtained by the Pep Club and has been a boost to the spirit of Vol supporters."

A L'il Abner motif on September 26, 1953, after Smokey I seemed to win the hearts of the Tennessee faithful at halftime of the game with Mississippi State. He became the mascot officially at the Duke game on October 3. Shown with Smoky I are Wes Pritchard, from Cleveland, Tennessee, Ruth Ann Barker from Humboldt, Tennessee, and Diane Darning, from Knoxville, Tennessee. Courtesy U.T. Photographic Services.

From these humble beginnings, Smokey has become part of a grand and still evolving tradition among Vol fans. The names of Reverend Bill Brooks and Stuart Worden, and later Earl Hudson, are not considered watchwords in U.T. history, but they should be. They were (and are) the moving forces behind the mascot becoming and remaining a campus reality.

They join the brothers of Alpha Gamma Rho, a fraternity on campus since 1951 and Smokey's handlers since 1977, in helping build Smokey's legend.

"These are dogs, you know," an editorial from September 24, 1953, in the *Orange and White* stated, "who possess the 'personality, spirit, appearance, and vitality' which the Pep Club seeks, and, if this one does, it does not seem far-fetched that he may play a major part in that modern-day miracle—a revival of U-T school spirit."

The history of the Smokeys is subject to vagaries of memory and the recollections of the participants of that time, errors, exaggerations, and interpretations not based on many facts. Earl Hudson, who knows more about these dogs and their history than anyone alive, admits that selection of Smokey I is "as much legend as it is fact."

"Most books aren't that exact about Smokey," agrees Earl's brother, Y. C. Hudson.

The next chapter will lay out what we do know about the world the new mascot was born into—it seems to be both a far-off country, long ago, yet deeply familiar.

3

THE 1953 UNIVERSITY OF TENNESSEE CAMPUS SCENE: A MUCH KINDER AND GENTLER PLACE

"The 1953–1954 school year has been a significant period in the history of the University. It was a year of increasing enrollment, of achievement on the part of students and faculty alike, and of noticeable changes in the physical appearance of the University campus."

> —Dr. C. E. Brehm, President, University of Tennessee,
> 1953–54 *Volunteer* Yearbook

The University of Tennessee campus in the early 1950s was tightly circumscribed around the "The Hill"—the oldest part of campus, with one building dating back to 1872—where most classes took place, Shields-Watkins Field (the precursor of today's Neyland Stadium, a Mecca of sorts on fall Saturday afternoons), the Lower Second Creek Valley, and the site of what is now called the Carolyn P. Brown Memorial Student Center at the corner of Cumberland Avenue and 15th Street, later Stadium Drive, now Phillip Fulmer Way.

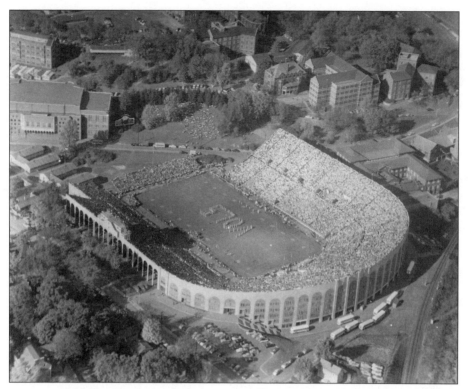

The early 1950s Shields-Watkins Field shown filled to capacity. Courtesy U.T. Photographic Services.

No observer of campus can fail to notice, despite the school's love for tradition, how often building and street names change. Many of those buildings remain today, many rehabilitated, many serving different functions than before. Alas, Science Hall on The Hill is no longer with us, a victim of a ravaging and memorable fire in the 1960s.

Campus life in the mid-fifties proceeded at a leisurely pace. "Enrollment was less than half of what it is now," said Lenoir City, Tennessee, lawyer Harvey Sproul, then vice-president of the Pep Club and editor of the *Orange and White*, the student newspaper that eventually became the *Daily Beacon* in 1965.

"Students didn't congregate that much around the strip. Ellis & Ernest and Byerley's Cafeteria were right there. The campus was less cosmopolitan, you might say, steeped in the old traditions. I suspect World War II had really slowed down a lot of the traditions."

Science Hall was a definite landmark on the Hill before being destroyed by fire in the mid-1960s. Courtesy U.T. Libraries, Special Collections.

The student newspaper was a breathless compendium of campus life, with opinion columns, campus gossip, news about elections, and all the other happenings on campus the editors deemed important. "Unofficial news spread quickly as students used Ellis and Ernest, Byerley's and the T-Room for eating and gathering," wrote Betsey Beeler Creekmore in 1994.[1]

There were residences, businesses, and churches in the area to the west of the campus and the stadium area, with streets named South Seventeenth, Yale, Rose, Detroit, and Cornell Avenues. The residents, many of whom were on the faculty, considered it a great place to live.

The Carousel Theatre on South Seventeenth Street was right in the midst of it all. The Armory-Fieldhouse on Yale Avenue had not yet been built. It would become part of the campus scene for the 1958–59 basketball season, with seating for 7,500 fans. In 1966–67, it would be expanded to 12,700 seats and be named Stokely Athletics Center. Calvary Baptist Church, with a large rock (now a target of student expression and moved across the street) in its parking lot, was next door.

The Louisville and Nashville train station in the area, just a few miles west of the main station downtown, was known as "West Knoxville." Unlike today, there wasn't much of the city past that area. Traveling to Farragut, west of Knoxville and on the main drag to Nashville, was an all-day trip.

A look at the advertisers in the *Orange and White* and in the *Volunteer* recalls some famous Knoxville names. Paul Dean's Toggery was at 1643 W. Cumberland, phone 5–3337; Knoxville phone numbers had not yet progressed into seven digits. Ellis & Ernest Drugs was on the "west side" of campus, complete with the Vol Book Exchange in the back. That famed campus landmark would last until November 18, 1967, the day *News Sentinel* sports editor Tom Siler termed "historic on two counts." Tennessee knocked off Ole Miss 20–7 for the first time since 1958 at the new Memphis Memorial Stadium, and "Doc Ernest closed his campus drug store, the traditional gathering place of student and alums since the 1920s." Siler wrote that this had happened since "Doc Ernest," as he was known to the student body, was "under duress" from the university.

Son Hal Ernest said in March 2012 that the "duress" was not the university's purchase of the building as part of the extension of the lawn area of the student center, but rather the impact of closing the drug store he had run since 1926, working ten hours a day, six days a week. He had a heart attack the Wednesday or Thursday, Hal said, before the Tulane football game on November 11 at Neyland Stadium. "Closing the store," Hal said, "caused that much emotional stress." The senior Ernest died on July 11, 1982.

There was the Sterling House, 609–11 Market Street, offering Dorothy Korby striped blouses in white/black and white/red for $5.95, worth around $48.00 in 2010. Hall's was at 318 S. Gay Street, offering Arrow Golden Oxford Shirts for $5.00, worth around $40.00 in 2010. Miller's Department Store downtown offered jackets for $11.85, vests for $1.77, suit hangers for 88 cents, and leather billfolds for $2.88.

There was an ad for Lucky Strike cigarettes, offering students the chance to make $25.00 by writing a jingle, based on the premise that Luckies taste better. Not to be outdone, there was an ad for Camel cigarettes that featured New York Yankees star outfielder Mickey Mantle.

Byerley's Restaurant had a suggestion for that dinner date: "Take Her to Byerley's. Near the Campus." Regas Restaurant on Gay at Magnolia sent out a message of "Welcome Freshmen." There was Highlands Grill, 3800 Kingston Pike, highlighting a "Frosh Mixer."

The University of Tennessee Book Store had its ad touting its location, "On Top of the Hill . . . for your convenience." There was a new book called the *Herman Hickman Reader*, authored by the famed Vol lineman (1929–31), College Football Hall of Fame member, head coach at Yale, and raconteur, offered from Simon and Schuster at $2.95 each.

In 1963, land acquisition began in the area between 15th Street and the railroad was part of the Yale Avenue Urban Renewal Project at a cost of $2.8 million, an area covering 135 acres in which more than 393 families were relocated and 341 buildings demolished. The Carousel Theatre survived the wrecking ball, but precious few other campus and neighborhood landmarks did.

A U.T. administrator named Dr. Edward J. Boling, who would be named the school's president in 1970, seized upon features of national urban renewal legislation—much of it since repealed—to accomplish this unprecedented growth westward on campus. This area is now home to fraternity houses, dormitories, classrooms, the John C. Hodges Library, and a host of athletic facilities.

In 1953, Shields-Watkins Field (it didn't become Neyland Stadium until 1962) had seating for 46,000 fans, with the lower deck on the east, south, and west sides and bleachers at the north end, but was rarely filled to capacity.

Looking back at game-day photos from those days, it seems strange to see empty seats all across the stadium. There was also what passed for a press box, but it pales in comparison to those found in college football stadiums today.

Lights were nearly twenty years away from becoming a fixture at the stadium, arriving in 1972. Even with much-lower stands on the west side, the late-afternoon shadows from the press box were often troublesome.

The field had a scoreboard on The Hill at the north end, complete with a clock that was really a clock, with minute and second hands. There were a number of fans who found vantage points on The Hill, since from that angle a fan could watch most of the game without having to pay for a ticket.

Since the official attendance figures began to be tallied in 1946, the Vols had averaged more than 30,000 fans in the seats only three times between that year and 1953. two of those years occurred in 1948 and 1949, after the expansion at the south end that made the stadium a horseshoe. From 1950 through 1952, Tennessee teams played to average crowds of 24,910, 23,961, and 27,321, respectively. They played in three bowl games, and the 1950 and 1951 teams are considered among the best in school history. The 1953 team would play in front of a total of 128,440 fans at home, 21,406 on an average Saturday.

The Vols would not crack the 40,000 average attendance mark until 1965, and that came three years after an expansion on the west side, a new upper deck and press box.

Due to treacherous mountain roads to the east, west, and north, the trip to Knoxville from anywhere outside fifty miles or so in those pre-interstate days could be a killer, although many students and football fans made the trips to and from Knoxville with regularity. For many others, Nashville and Memphis might well have been in another country.

There were other challenges facing the university, challenges that would be met head-on in the 1960s.

Rumblings of desegregating campus life were starting to be heard, much to the displeasure of campus higher-ups and media across the state. It was a year before the U.S. Supreme Court's landmark decision in *Brown v. Board of Education of Topeka* of May 1954. The *Tennessean*, Nashville's morning newspaper, then as now the most influential newspaper in the state, had run an editorial on September 28, 1950, expressing the opinion that "mixed education was unwise for both races."

In April 1953, Andy Holt, assistant to president Dr. Cloide Everett Brehm and later the university's president from 1959 to 1970, expressed a popular belief that the restrictions based on race would work no hardships on African-American students: "Negroes prefer to attend school with people of their own race," he said.[2]

In her 1994 history of the university, Betsey Beeler Creekmore reported that tentative steps toward desegregating the campus had been taken, a year earlier and a year later. "[In 1952], Eugene Mitchell Gray, Knoxville College graduate, became the first black student to be enrolled on campus as the trustees complied with a court order to admit black students to the graduate school and College of Law. Lilly Jenkins was the first black person to receive a UT campus degree, the master's in special education, in 1954."[3]

Still, the prospect of African American students on campus troubled uncertain white Tennesseans, on campus and across the state.

THE PATH TO A
DESEGREGATED CAMPUS

On January 4, 1961, undergraduate students Theotis Robinson Jr., Charles Edgar Blair, and Willie Mae Gillespie were admitted to the University of Tennessee, culminating a series of legal battles to admit African American students that stretched back into the late 1930s. University Historian Dr. Milton Klein provided a cogent analysis of the way that all finally came about.

> During the summer of 1960, while Knoxville's African-American community was demonstrating to desegregate downtown restaurants and lunch counters. Theotis Robinson, a black graduate of [Knoxville's] Austin High School, sought admission to UT's undergraduate school. The application was rejected: Robinson persisted and secured an interview with the university's president, Andrew Holt. Holt expressed ignorance of the university's policies with regard to undergraduate admission of blacks but promised to take the matter up with the Board of Trustees. Robinson agreed but warned that if the Board did not change its policies, he would file a lawsuit against the university. The state attorney general advised the recalcitrant trustees that in view of the Tennessee Supreme Court's decision in *Roy v. Brittain*, the university could not deny Robinson's application. The board thereupon capitulated, and on Nov. 18, 1960, adopted a resolution: 'That it is the policy of the Board that there shall be no racial discrimination in the admission of qualified students to the University of Tennessee.'[4]

That meeting took place the day before the football home season finale against Kentucky.

Desegregating the University of Tennessee athletic program was another story. In September 1953, nearly seven years had elapsed since Tennessee had forfeited a December 23, 1946, basketball game against Duquesne University, rather than play against a team that refused to bench an African American player. Head coach John Mauer "polled" his team and told media the team "voted not to play."

The Associated Press reported the decision not to play the game in a wire story in the *Knoxville Journal* on December 24, 1946. The game is not mentioned in the "Results Section" in the 2012 *Tennessee Basketball Media Guide,* nor is the game mentioned in *The Basketball Vols,* written by Ben Byrd in 1974, the most recent history of the Vol basketball program. While the game was listed in the *Knoxville Journal* and in Tennessee game programs as being in Pittsburgh, the dateline on the AP story was McKeesport, Pennsylvania. The University of Tennessee Sports Information Office file of basketball scorebooks shows the pages for the Duquesne game filled out with the names of the officials, but not listing players on either team.

In 1967–68, history was in one of its cycles of change. Nashville's Lester McClain had come to Knoxville as a scholarship athlete thirteen years after the Supreme Court's *Brown vs. Board of Education* decision and a year after the University of Kentucky had signed Greg Page and Nat Northington in football and Vanderbilt had likewise inked Perry Wallace in basketball.

Head coach Doug Dickey led the way for the Vols, saying the time was right to make the move. The times then may have been troubled and uncertain, but it is worth remembering that, when this significant social advance was made, a number of brave people, in this case McClain, Dickey, Condredge Holloway, Bill Battle, and the late Jimmy Streater, led the way.

McClain had been one of two African American players the Vols had recruited in the 1966–67 season. The other, fullback Albert Davis of Alcoa (often referred to in Knoxville media reports of the day as "Alcoa's great Negro running back"), was not admitted to the university, so the torch passed to McClain.

Sports Illustrated's Dan Jenkins covered Tennessee's 1968 football season opener against Georgia at Neyland Stadium (Tennessee 17, Georgia 17) and this piece of prose came though his fingers and onto the pages of the September 23, 1968, issue in an article entitled "A Rouser on a Rug." The story centered on the new Tartan turf on the floor of Shields-Watkins Field, but raised other issues as well. Sadly, there was brief mention of Uga, but none of Smokey.

> There at the end, with Tennessee quarterback Bubba Wyche throwing a touchdown pass and then a two-point conversion after the clock had run out, everything was sagging, especially heartbeats, but not the gleaming nylon playing field. It was still a rich green and as spotless as it was when the game began three hours earlier. And this was after a truckload of Tennessee cheerleaders had driven on it, after a Georgia bulldog had

Wide receiver Lester McClain was the first African-American player at Tennessee, making his varsity debut in the 1968 Georgia game. U.T. Sports Information Office.

Albert Davis, star fullback for Alcoa High School, was also recruited during the 1966–67 season. Shown here at his signing, the offer of admission was later rescinded under controversial circumstances. Davis returned to U.T. to earn a master's degree. Standing behind Davis are Assistant Coach Jimmy Dunn, Head Coach Doug Dickey, and Athletics Director Bob Woodruff. U.T. Sports Information Office.

gnawed on it and after a Georgia coach had flicked ashes from his pipe on it. It was even after a Negro had played on it, which hasn't happened every day in the Southeastern Conference. The verdict so far has to be that God blew it when he gave us grass.

McClain finished his Vol career in 1970 with 70 career catches for 1,003 yards and 10 touchdowns, and was on the receiving end of an 82-yard TD reception from quarterback Bobby Scott in the 1969 Memphis State game.

After his career had ended, McClain told writers covering the Vol football program he was determined to make the best of things, despite a rough patch or two along the way.

"There is a time you question whether you want to pack your bags and go home," McClain said. "I would be lying if I said I never considered that. But I just couldn't. I knew the next day the headlines would say, 'Lester McClain, first black athlete, quits U.T.'" McClain ended up being the trailblazer, and history records his contributions to the Vol program, on and off the field.

As for Davis, Dr. Klein wrote in *Volunteer Moments* that "Controversy surrounding the conditions of his recruitment caused the University to rescind its offer to the young Alcoa star June 15, 1967, causing embarrassment to both Davis and the University."

For his part, Davis recounted the affair in an August 5, 1992, interview for the U.T. Oral History Project, the interview conducted by Robert Eppling.

The SEC did not have any ball players that were black on the basketball, football, athletics. The pressure was coming in on them from that aspect. They wanted to do something about it, but their supporters somewhere down the line didn't want that right then. I got caught up in that. If I was so dumb as they say, and I couldn't do this, then why do I have a degree from the University of Tennessee? See what I'm saying? My master's degree. I finished four years at Tennessee State, BS degree, and a master's from the University of Tennessee. . . . And then to go to the University of Tennessee, and then it's a big thing you know, "He didn't pass the test." That's a lie. I never did take the test to go to the University of Tennessee. The truth is, you told me at the University of Tennessee, the AD said, "You cannot go to school here. You cannot walk on. You cannot pay your own way." That is the truth. The president said, "we accept you and your SAT." That's what was told to me.

As president from 1959 to 1970, Dr. Holt, a native of Milan, Tennessee, would lead the amazing growth of the campus in the mid-1960s, when the post-World War II baby boom children had grown and started coming to college and the flagship campus of the university was opened to all who could qualify.

He would become a revered campus figure to those who knew him over the years. He combined a folksy, "down home" exterior with a shrewd political mind that made him a formidable foe for those who had to deal with him, particularly in the Tennessee General Assembly.

Including Dr. Holt (whose name graces Andy Holt Tower, for example, on the Knoxville campus), several professors and administrators of the time around 1953 have their names affixed on buildings across the expanse of campus in Knoxville, well beyond Ayres Hall. Lexemuel Ray Hesler, for example, was Dean of Liberal Arts, and the Biology Building is now named in his honor.

Dr. Nathan Washington Dougherty, captain of the 1909 football team and known in his campus days as "Big 'Un," was mistakenly listed in the 1953–54 Volunteer as Nathan A. Dougherty. He was head of engineering, with the Engineering Building on the Hill now named in his honor and memory. James D. Hoskins was President Emeritus, having had his name affixed to what was then the "main library," as it was known for many years, located on Cumberland Avenue, in 1950.

Jessie L. Harris, Vice-Dean of Home Economics, now has the Jessie Harris Building at the corner of Cumberland and 13th Street named in her honor for students of human ecology. Ralph Dunford, the namesake of Dunford Hall, was Dean of Men.

The campus did attract national attention.

Los Angeles Times reporter Jeff Prugh came to Knoxville to cover the 1968 football game with UCLA and left with some major impressions of campus life that reflected the tenor of the late sixties. Prugh compared the Tennessee campus with others around the country, calling Knoxville campus a "place where kids listen instead of shout, where coats and ties have scored a smashing victory over beads and bare feet." But Prugh also focused on the time that had preceded it—and the central part of our story.

Dr. Klein wrote that Prugh "went to great lengths" to point out that the most controversial subject on the Knoxville campus had been the decision to choose between a Tennessee Walking Horse or a coonhound as the school's mascot. That event had happened fifteen years earlier, but Dr. Klein still believed it had an impact, reflecting the tone of campus life in those days.[5]

Andy Holt served as president of the University of Tennessee from 1959 through 1970, leading the institution's growth and development. Courtesy U.T. Photographic Services.

4

THE TIDE OF TIMES IN TENNESSEE FOOTBALL, 1953: NEVER FOLLOW A LEGEND

"On the first page of the survival manual for coaches is this firm rule: Politely turn down all opportunities to replace great coaches. Repeat: *Do not follow famous footprints.* Harvey Robinson did not really want to be head coach at Tennessee but failed to heed that fundamental warning when Gen. Robert R. Neyland gave up coaching (but remained athletic director) after the 1952 season."

—**Marvin West,** *Tales of the Tennessee Vols,* 13

Just as the campus was a very different place in 1953 and experiencing long-lasting changes, so was Tennessee football. As the season began, Gen. Robert R. Neyland had turned over the reins of the Vol program to Assistant Coach Harvey Robinson, a Weaverville, North Carolina, native and letterman from the 1931–32 teams. Often called "Robbie," he made his debut as a head coach in the 1953 season opener against Mississippi State on September 26, 1963, albeit a 26–0 loss.[1]

In that momentous year of 1953, the Vol football program would begin the tentative steps of establishing an identity beyond the towering personality of General Neyland. That process would take more than ten years, with a number of stops and starts over that time, leading to finally dropping Tennessee's famous single-wing offensive formation in 1964, two years after General Neyland had died.

The University of Tennessee's 1953 schedule, as sponsored by Tennessee Mill & Mine Supply, Inc. Earl Hudson collection.

The season was the first on The Hill without Gen. Neyland on the east sideline of Shields-Watkins Field since 1926, except for his tours of duty in Panama in 1935 and in World War II from 1941 to 1945. He was coach from 1926 to 1934, from 1936 to 1940, and from 1946–52 before stepping down. His was a legendary tenure. General Neyland had "made" Tennessee football, his time on campus bringing a legacy of winning. Here's what one Tennessee historian had to say about General Neyland:

> It is evident from all accounts that Neyland had a towering, dominating, and even intimidating presence. Taciturn in demeanor and seeking excellence on all fronts, Neyland's impact on collegiate football was felt across the South and the nation. Today, he is revered by those who played for him, respected by those who coached against him, and, more than 40 years after his death, honored as his name and legacy live on.

General Neyland compiled a 173-31-12 record in three tenures at the University of Tennessee. U.T. Sports Information Office.

In a 1969 poll, a panel of 100 experts named Neyland the number 2 coach of all time, second only to Knute Rockne. This accolade came 17 years after Neyland had hung up his whistle and seven years after his death.[2]

The year did not get off to a great start. Ranked number 8 at the end of Neyland's last season by the Associated Press, the Vols endured a 16–0 defeat at the hands of number 10 Texas in the January 1 Cotton Bowl. Coupled with Neyland's departure (even though many thought it was possibly temporary), fans' spirits were dampened considerably.

General Neyland had been rumored to be in ill health during the 1952 season, and players of that day, most notably fullback Andy Kozar, have confirmed it. His doctors would not allow him to coach in the Cotton Bowl against Texas, so he had stepped down in December that season for health reasons, turning the team over to Robinson. The Cotton Bowl game, however, was credited to the General's coaching dossier.

Many dignitaries sensed momentous changes were on the way, and tributes were due. On August 18, 1953, Neyland was honored with a testimonial dinner at Cherokee Country Club, featuring U.S. Rep. Howard Baker Sr., Sens. Albert Gore and Estes Kefauver, Gov. Frank Clement, sportswriter Grantland Rice, and a host of former players, including Bobby Dodd, Gene McEver, Beattie Feathers, Harry (Hobo) Thayer, Murray Warmath, Bowden Wyatt, and Herman (Breezy) Wynn.

For his part, Robinson seemed to be coaching with a short stick—beginning with a new rule engineered by none other than Neyland himself as chair of the NCAA Rules Committee. He had forced through a major change from two-platoon football to players who had to play both defense and offense. General Neyland had once termed the two-platoon game "chickenshit football." Lindsey Nelson recalled Neyland making that statement in his autobiography.[3] In his more eloquent moments, Neyland called it "rat race football."

Harvey Robinson followed General Neyland as head coach in 1953 and 1954, with a 10-10-1 record. He is shown here with tailback Tom Tracy (86) and quarterback Hal Hubbard (19). *Knoxville News Sentinel.*

While there was disagreement on the NCAA rules committee about this change, Neyland, as chairman, had his way, as he usually did, regardless of the impact it might have on the fortunes of the Tennessee Vols.

In preseason commentary in the 1953 *Tennessee Football Media Guide,* Robinson indicated that he believed he had been dealt a bad hand from the beginning. "The outlook for the 1953 season is discouraging, but not hopeless. We are faced with the additional task of converting offense to defense and defense to offense. This, of course, is an impossibility when we are restricted to a twenty-day practice period." Bob Gilbert wrote that Robinson "found it difficult to convert 'specialists' to single-platoon football—to teach them to play offense and defense."[4]

Tom Siler wrote that Robinson faced a "thankless" task in replacing General Neyland. Noting that Robinson had a "keen and analytical football mind," Siler nevertheless reported that Robbie and top aide Farmer Johnson did not agree how to play. "Harvey made basic changes in the famed six-man defense which was Neyland's own brainchild." That led to friction within the staff, but Siler reported that, "Johnson objected in vain."[5]

Joe Harb, sports editor of the 1953–54 *Volunteer,* wrote, "The squad was severely handicapped by graduation and with the changing over to the one-platoon system an additional burden was put on the coaching staff . . . [We] of the student body know [Robinson] will continue to produce the best teams possible."

The Vols were coming of a three-year run of 27 wins, only 4 losses, and 1 tie from 1950 to 1952. They won national championships in 1950 and 1951 and produced more great players in that period than anybody could ever have imagined. It was the last of General Neyland's three great eras of coaching Tennessee football.[6]

With the very imposing presence of General Neyland looming just down the hall in the Athletic Association offices in South Stadium and the loss of many of the talented players who had led the way from 1950 to 1952, the Vol football program fell on hard times, leading to records of 6–4-1 (a "remarkable accomplishment," Siler wrote) in 1953 and 4–6 in 1954.

One of the major highlights of the 1953 season, other than a scoreless tie against perennial rival Alabama (in the only televised game of the season and only the third televised game ever for the Vols), was defensive back Ray Martin of Danville, Virginia, pilfering a pass from Louisville quarterback Johnny

Unitas and returning it 100 yards for a score. Martin gained more yardage on a single return than Morris Vowell (99 yards) against Sewanee in 1916, Eric Berry at Florida in 2007 or Conrad Graham against Memphis State in 1972, each 96 yards, or Shaun Ellis's 90 yards at Auburn in 1998.

Tennessee started off the 1954 season 4–2, but tailed off badly, losing the final four games to Georgia Tech, Florida, Kentucky, and Vanderbilt, respectively. The Vandy game in Nashville was a 26–0 loss, a contest highlighted by a number of brawls on the field. Russ Bebb wrote that "Bloodthirsty Commodore fans, unaccustomed as they were to beating Tennessee, yelled in unison as the Vols lined up to kickoff in the second half: 'Block that kick! Block that kick!'"[7]

Thus did Robinson's tenure at Tennessee begin and end with 26–0 losses. In late November 1954, Athletic Director Neyland dismissed Robinson and his staff.

"Four days after his '54 team had been battered by Vanderbilt," the *Journal*'s Ed Harris wrote, "Robinson was to read in the *Knoxville Journal* of his dismissal and all his staff."

"I hate to read that," General Neyland said after receiving a copy of the story from Harris at a Vol basketball game. "I just didn't know how to handle the situation. It was the first time I ever had to do anything to hurt any of my boys." Neyland later said that dismissing Robinson and his staff was the "hardest thing I ever had to do." To make matters worse, the 1954 staff mostly comprised former Tennessee Vols.[8]

Col. Tom Elam, the legendary trustee and athletics board member from Union City, Tennessee, had told sportswriter Al Browning that he foresaw an "unsettling transition" in Tennessee football. "The end came for Robinson after our loss to Georgia Tech in Atlanta in 1954," he said. "I was walking from the hotel to the stadium with Neyland. Even before that game, he mentioned a change was coming. I think he or his representatives were talking with Bowden Wyatt by then."[9]

Ever the loyal soldier ("I didn't ask for the job. I didn't want to be head coach. I accepted because the General asked me to do so,") Robinson went to Florida as an assistant coach under former Tennessee tackle Bob Woodruff (1936–38) and returned to Tennessee in 1960 as backfield coach under Neyland protégé Bowden Wyatt, serving until 1963.[10]

Wyatt, a Kingston native, captain of the 11–0 1938 team, and an All-America selection that season, came marching home to Knoxville in January 1955. "It's been a rough decision for me," Wyatt said, "but I'm going back to the job I've always wanted." When the job had opened up in late 1954, there was really only one candidate, at least according to public opinion. Neither Wyatt nor Colonel Elam, nor anyone else, could have realized how difficult the transition from under Neyland's shadow would be.[11]

Bowden Wyatt possessed movie star good looks and is one of the legends of Tennessee football. During his coaching career, he became one of only a handful of coaches who would win championships in three different conferences, first at Wyoming in the Big Sky Conference, then at Arkansas in the Southwestern Conference, and finally at Tennessee in the Southeastern Conference. Wyatt appeared at the Tennessee football banquet on January 13, 1955, and was introduced to a smallish crowd outside the U.T. Student Center

Bowden Wyatt talks with University of Tennessee students at the Student Center in January 1955 shortly after being named head coach. U.T. Sports Information Office.

the next day. He won the SEC title at Tennessee in his second year, but fell on hard times two years later and never recovered.

Wyatt, one of only three men inducted into the College Football Hall of Fame as a player and a coach, would cling grimly to the beloved single-wing, even though prep prospects across the nation and even the state, prime examples being quarterbacks Steve Spurrier in Johnson City and Steve Sloan in Cleveland, chose to go elsewhere, showcasing their passing talents in some variant of the T formation.

It was a messy situation for the Tennessee leadership and family, made harder that a Tennessee legend was involved. Marvin West recounted what

Bowden Wyatt came to Tennessee after winning conference champion-ships at Wyoming and Arkansas. U.T. Sports Information Office.

happened. "He failed to recognize new academic demands and lost key players each year. The loss of key aide and long-time confidant Dick Hitt weighed heavily. Wyatt's problem with alcohol was the other major factor in his downfall. Pushing Birmingham columnist Alf Van Hoose, fully clothed, into a swimming pool at a conference meeting may have been the proverbial last straw."[12]

Others weighed in with similar sentiments.

"My own belief is that Wyatt's downfall at Tennessee was due principally to his failure to assess the true situation there before Neyland's death," Fred Russell of the *Nashville Banner* wrote after Wyatt's death. "Bowden couldn't seem to realize that there were many people within the Tennessee administration and faculty who resented General Neyland's dominance and were bent on correcting it. At no other great institution perhaps had a coach and athletic director become so powerful in the affairs in the university. With the general's death, this had to end. It was in the cards. But Wyatt, so long exposed to the Neyland image and influence, couldn't adjust."[13]

He was never again a head coach, but was an assistant coach for a couple of years at Oklahoma State, thanks to a helping hand from Alabama head coach Bear Bryant. After two years, he went into business in Knoxville.

Wyatt died—suddenly, Russ Bebb wrote—of intestinal flu early in the morning on January 21, 1969, in Sweetwater, Tennessee.

It was thus a time of a very long transition beginning in 1953, as General Neyland's history-making coaching career came to an end, with 173 wins, 31 losses, and 12 ties, in three different eras as the leader of the Vol football program.

With the Vol program facing life without General Neyland, there was another change that, over the years, would inspire as many myths and as much devotion as General Neyland's legendary reign: the selection of a mascot.

Here's how it transpired.

5

THE BLUETICK COMETH

Talk about humble beginnings. The search for a mascot began just two years after the national championship season of 1951, as campus student leaders attempted to create some excitement about UT football.

The task facing members of the U.T. Pep Club, led by Fountain City resident Stuart Worden, then twenty-one years old, was certainly a daunting one for a group of youthful college students. They were completely absorbed in selecting a mascot, but didn't have any idea they were contributing to history.

The idea grew out of the ambience of their college days, an effort to breathe spirit into the daily life of the university at that time. The main players in the evolving drama were a colorful lot.

Rev. W. C. Brooks, forty-two, referred to in early newspaper accounts to as "Bill" or "Willie," was an Army veteran living in the John Sevier community of Knox County just off Rutledge Pike, known as "Bloody 11W" in later years, across the street from John Sevier Baptist Church. He had founded and owned "Bill's Clutch Shop" in the neighborhood and was raising Blueticks. Reverend Brooks was also the head of missions for the Knox County Baptist Association. He had, by Earl Hudson's recollection, "spent a lot of time building new churches in West Virginia, Montana, North and South Dakota, and in Bolivia. He was a lay minister who did a lot of good for a lot of people."

Stuart Worden was a popular student leader often referred to in campus media as "Stu" or "Stu-baby." He dismissed the nicknames as "something college students do." He was a business major and University of Tennessee Pep Club president, leading the process of selecting the mascot. Worden was

Bill Brooks owned this clutch shop on Rutledge Pike (now Old Rutledge Pike) near his home. It was originally called "Bill's Clutch Shop," later named "Southern Clutch & Supply" after Reverend Brooks retired. Tom Mattingly.

described by one of his campus colleagues as "just about the most enthusiastic person you'll ever meet, even if he is afflicted with hay fever." Today, Worden is senior partner of Worden, Rechenbach, & Brooke, a firm specializing in financial planning, investments, and insurance, with offices on Gay Street in Knoxville.

For his part, at this time Earl Hudson owned a drug store on North Broadway at Woodland Avenue in Knoxville. Hudson, Worden, and Reverend Brooks became the principal architects in bringing a mascot named "Brooks' Blue Smokey" and eight others with similar-sounding names into the annals of the University of Tennessee history.

For context, here's what was happening outside the confines of the U.T. campus in Knoxville.

The year 1953 saw the growth of the buy now pay later mentality with car makers leading the way by allowing longer and longer periods to pay for your new car. Queen Elizabeth II crowned queen of England.

The unions gained strength with more and more workers belonging to unions, with wage and price controls ended and unemployment at 2.9 percent the increases in standard of living continued to grow and appear to have no boundaries. A teacher's average salary was $4,254, and a pound of round steak was 90 cents. The first color television sets appear, selling for $1,175, and transistor radios start to appear for sale.

"No Other Love," sung by Perry Como, had been number 1 on the record charts since August 15. "You, You, You," by the Ames Brothers, followed for two weeks in late September. The dominant songs of the year had been Como's "Don't Let the Stars Get in Your Eyes," "The Doggie in the Window" by Patti Page, and "Song From Moulin Rouge" by Percy Faith.[1]

Author Peter Golenbock had his own take on the year.

Through the winter of 1952 the Korean War continued to rage, and into the spring of 1953 there were reports of peace talks, but these reports had been alluded to since the middle of 1951, and the people at home were getting tired of ballooned hopes and then disillusionment. Twenty-three thousand Americans were dead and 70,000 wounded. At the U.N. Dag Hammerskjold replaced Trygve Lee. McCarthyism was peaking as the Justice Department refused to allow comedian Charley Chaplin's return to the country without investigating him for subversion and moral turpitude. Chaplin stayed in Switzerland. Eddie Fisher sang at the Paramount Theatre, cofeatured with Vincent Price's *House of Wax*.[2]

In Knoxville, the 1953 school year began with the announcement in local media that the Pep Club was holding a contest to pick not only a mascot, but to name it as well. In the first issue of the *Orange and White,* on Thursday, September 24, a headline entitled "Holt and Waters Named U-T Veeps by Trustees Board" competed with one that said, "Pep Club Seeks Dog as Mascot." Andy Holt and Eugene Waters, respectively, were the two appointees, with the former to become much better known than the latter. The story indicated that Dr. Holt's duties were "largely administrative in assisting the president," while Dr. Waters's were "academic, dealing with the faculty." In the page 1 story on the Pep Club's plans, without a byline, the writer noted that "U-T has been one of the few major universities without a mascot."

In another front-page story, President Dr. C. E. Brehm proposed spending $13.5 million on a variety of projects, including $2 million for an "armory and fieldhouse," $1 million for a geology and physics building, $2 million to replace Estabrook Hall, and thirteen other projects in Knoxville and Martin.

The mascot search had also been featured in both Knoxville newspapers on the previous Sunday, September 20. The *Knoxville Journal* story carried the byline of John Ward, the youthful journalist and broadcaster who would do live Tennessee basketball play-by-play in 1954 from Alumni Gymnasium on the Hill on WTSK Television. He had already been referred to in print as John ("The Voice") Ward.[3] (In ensuing years, starting in 1965 in basketball and 1968 in football, Ward would become a beloved figure around the expanse of Big Orange Country, telling the story of Tennessee athletics on radio broadcasts and coaches' shows. He would be much in demand as a speaker wherever Vol fans gathered.) The *News Sentinel* story appeared without a byline, mentioning

An early shot of the Vol Network. From left (top) are Edwin Huster Sr., lead broadcaster George Mooney, and spotter Julian Andes. Analyst Bob Foxx is at the lower left. U.T. Sports Information Office.

in the lead that "It appears that University of Tennessee athletic teams are finally going to have a mascot—yes, a real live one." In a section of the story entitled "Symbol of History," the story went on to report that, "After much consideration and debate, and the approval of the school's All-Students Club, it was decided that a 'hound dog is to represent Tennessee's colors.'"

The decision "stemmed from the fact that most of our ancestors, the ones who made Tennessee famous, were the sturdy, hardy, courageous pioneers. And whoever heard of a pioneer without an ever-faithful hound."

There had been signs all over campus about the mascot contest. "This can't be an ordinary hound. He must be a 'Houn Dawg' in the best sense," the signs read.

"We want a name which typifies the heritage of our state, which signifies the spirit and tradition of the Volunteer," Worden had said.

Worden had taken over as Pep Club president at the beginning of the 1953–54 school year, having been elected the preceding April. Despite the success of the Vol program since the start of the decade of the 1950s, he saw a problem.

"Student spirit was very, very weak," he said. "Gen. Neyland was a wonderful football coach, interested in football games and winning, but had the least interest in school spirit in our thoughts. We used to try to get him to come to pep rallies, and that didn't happen. I don't think I ever remember him coming to a pep rally. We were desperately trying to get more spirit around the games."

Looking back, the idea of needing to infuse life into the Tennessee fan base on and off campus seems strange, given the popularity of the Vol program over the years.

You might have thought that school spirit would have been the least of the concerns of the day, but it was. We've already recounted that the coaching staff and the fan base were in an uneasy period of transition after General Neyland had stepped down, and this no doubt had some effect on morale. The *Orange and White* carried a number of stories with fans having strong opinions on both sides of the school spirit issue.

Here's another recollection on the Neyland era recounted in September 1, 2010, issue of the Knoxville weekly newspaper *Metro Pulse* entitled "A Personal View of the Vols' Most Legendary Coach, Robert Neyland." Knoxvillian Jo Markelonis remembered working for General Neyland "back in her 20s," and recalled what those days in the early 1950s were like on campus. "When I was in school, there wasn't all that much to do, in the way of entertainment and time-killers." So she went to ball games. "Most students did, though it was so much smaller then. Neyland's Vols had their fans among alumni, as she recalls, but current UT students usually dominated the crowds. The more casual fans watched games sitting on the grass of the Hill."

Knoxville ad executive Hal Ernest, also a student at the time, had a similar, but slightly different, perspective on the times. "When General Neyland came back from World War II," he said, "there was a sparse crowd for a pep rally before the 1946 Georgia Tech game. After that, he said 'I'd never come back.'"

Ernest, like Worden an important student on campus, was steadfast in his desire to have Neyland appear at a pep rally before the 1952 Alabama game. When he asked Neyland assistant Edna Callaway, the business manager of athletics, about whether the General might attend, she said Neyland was "pretty sick." That did not dissuade him in the least.

He found a way to talk to the General and asked him directly if he could appear. In Ernest's retelling, the General replied, "I'm sick," he said. "My teeth are bad. I don't know if I could do that." Ernest insisted. The student body "loves and respects you. Please come."

What happened was this: Ernest rolled the dice and promoted Neyland's appearance all over campus, using a car and rented megaphone, appealing to the student body for its support.

"It was a beautiful night," he recalled. "It was crystal clear. The band and the cheerleaders were there. There was a bonfire. Everybody was into it."

There was one problem: no Gen. Neyland. The fire was dwindling. There were no more boxes. Things looked bad.

"Suddenly," Ernest said, "at the far end of the field, in the glow of the moonlight, there was a long, blue Cadillac. I was in a state of shock."

It was General Neyland.

Earnest continued: "He grabbed the microphone and talked and talked, recapping every Alabama game since 1928. I was astounded. He talked for thirty-five minutes. 'We're the underdogs,' he said, 'and we need you there tomorrow.'" Then he was gone.

Tennessee won the next day 20–0 over the number 18 Crimson Tide.

Despite this dramatic intervention, the essential problem remained the same: how to increase school spirit on campus. There was more to it than winning. Everybody seemed to have an idea. "We had representatives from around the campus on the Pep Club, and we would talk about different things, trying to figure out what to do to promote increased interest in the football games," Worden said. "The symbol of the university was the Vols, the Volunteer. It was a torch, nothing really to tie into. That was about all we had. Most of the other colleges and universities had some sort of a mascot."

So there was a buzz of activity among the Pep Club members, and a contest was set, with possibilities of all kinds on the table. "There were articles in the newspaper, with a request to send in recommendations for mascots," Worden said. "We got everything, about every animal you could think of. Everybody had their own ideas. The two that got the most comment were for some sort of a dog and the Tennessee Walking Horse." Ernest remembered that someone, he doesn't remember who, recommended a bear, a link to the Smoky Mountains. That suggestion did not seem to gain much traction.

It came down to those who wanted a mascot with the beauty and majesty of the Tennessee Walking Horse, balanced against those who wanted the more proletarian hound dog. The hound won out by vote of the Pep Club ("unanimously," as written in a Winter 1954 edition of the *Tennessee Alumnus*). So the stage was set for a contest to pick the best hound dog at halftime of the opening game of 1953.

But the Walking Horse lobby didn't go gently into that good night. There was a move made in the mid-1950s to replace the dog with a Tennessee Walking Horse.

Media reports indicated that Ike Green, a U.T. alum, working in concert with Newport industrialist M. M. Bullard, made an eloquent, if patronizing, appeal for the Walking Horse: "My idea is to replace old Smokey, the hound dog, with a beautiful spirited Tennessee Walking Horse which would lend more dignity and beauty to the half-time festivities at Shields-Watkins Field. You perhaps know that the Army has a goat for a mascot, and since Tennessee is known the world over as the home of the Tennessee Walker, I think it would be most appropriate to have the walking horse as our mascot. We are missing the boat by having a hound dog for a mascot when U-T could be represented by a Tennessee Walking Horse."

In succeeding years, the university, perhaps in response, began bringing a Walking Horse to games in Knoxville. That continued until the advent of artificial turf, since the horse could not safely negotiate sharp turns on fake grass. The horses stopped appearing at Neyland Stadium after the 1980 Georgia game.

The Athletic Department's Bud Ford handled the arrangements and remembered that a Walking Horse regularly appeared at Vols games in Nashville and Memphis, even at the dedication of a new stadium in Tampa in 1967. The horse also appeared at Grant Field in Atlanta, the Los Angeles Memorial Coliseum, the Gator Bowl, the Sugar Bowl, the Cotton Bowl, the Astro-Bluebonnet Bowl, the Florida Citrus Bowl, and the Sun Bowl.

With the return of grass in 1994, the Walking Horse, generally a Grand National Champion, has appeared on Homecoming Day.

In looking at the alternatives facing the Pep Club, as they debated the merits of a horse vs. a hound, Worden remembered that "one very smart member of the Pep Club" raised a cogent point. "How are we going to maintain and look after whatever mascot is chosen?" the unknown member said. "That's a live animal. Where is the money going to come from to feed, house, and make sure the mascot is there at the right time, home and away?"

Stuart Worden said it was "wonderful" to talk about having a mascot, but there were significant logistics involved. "There was a lot of pressure from various sources to choose the Tennessee Walking Horse as the mascot," he said, but with one major problem. "None of the Tennessee Walking Horse people offered any solutions on maintaining and supplying the horse in their proposals that I remember."

That seemed to foreclose that option. The local media weighed in, and a bold prediction was made in the September 24, 1953, edition of the *News Sentinel*. Outdoors writer Chambliss Pierce hinted strongly that Reverend Brooks's dog would be the front-runner, taking great care to spell the name correctly:

> Blue Smokey, a huge droopy-eared, sad-eyed blue tick coonhound, is picturesque as well as perfect, if you can say that about a dog. He's a showman by choice and as gentle as a four-point pledge. But he boasts a seven-generation pedigree and has twice won the Southeastern championship in addition to bench victories throughout Tennessee, Ohio and Indiana. And this is to say nothing about the countless coons who have suffered the hot breath of Smokey's chase. I know that is a lot of words to give a dog and I know a lot of friends have gotten less. But

This November 15, 1964, shot shows Smokey III getting acquainted with Tennessee Walking Horse named Mysterious Shadow of Franklin, Tennessee. Earl Hudson collection.

if Blue Smokey takes out on the field Saturday I want everyone to know they're looking at something special. And I'm sure a lot of coons and hunters would breathe a sigh of relief.

The day before the game, September 25, 1953, the *News Sentinel* indicated how the contest proceedings at the game would work. "One new and noisy event tomorrow afternoon will be the 'hound dawg' parade. All the floppy-eared candidates for All-Students mascot will be paraded one-by-one in front of the student section by cheerleaders. The dog garnering the most student applause thereby becomes the mascot, says Stuart Worden, president of the U-T Pep Club."

There was a picture a page earlier in that edition that might have led cynical observers to believe that the fix might be in. There was "Blue Smoky," pictured with two cheerleaders, Shirley Van Pelt and Dona Gardner. Captioned "VOL MASCOT CANDIDATE," the text read as follows: "Blue Smoky, owned by Rev. W. E [sic] Brooks, has been given to the University of Tennessee Pep Club for the Vol mascot contest. The hound dogs will be judged at tomorrow night's pep rally at the Rose Hole."

One thing is certain: Reverend Brooks was certainly not above engaging in a little self-promotion, looking for every angle he could to garner attention for his dog. He did feel confident about his chances, however, as Earl Hudson has explained. "I don't know if he knew he was going to win. He knew he had a good chance. Mildred felt the same way. She was pretty confident and knew Smokey would make a good mascot. It's hard to say who encouraged him to enter the contest. He did have some reservations." From Worden's point of

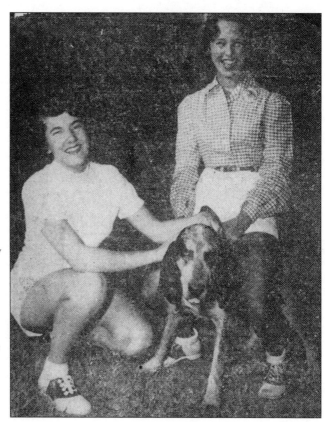

"Blue Smoky" is shown with U.T. cheerleaders Shirley Van Pelt (left) and Dona Gardner a few days before the contest held September 26, 1953. The caption indicated that Blue Smoky had been "given" to the University of Tennessee Pep Club by Reverend Brooks. *Knoxville News Sentinel* photo by Mickey Creager.

view, he said, "Reverend Brooks was the front-runner, without question. He had the dog and would do everything. He really made a big difference in our decision."

The Rose Hole was a vacant area behind the current Law School site, where fraternity and sorority members played softball and had pep rallies, complete with a bonfire. The name was a take-off on Pasadena's Rose Bowl, according to Ernest.

There is no evidence in either the *News Sentinel* or the *Journal* that the dogs actually did appear at the pep rally. The dogs did, however, appear at Shields-Watkins Field the next day.

September 26 finally arrived, with Mississippi State in town for the season opener. State's head coach was another former Vol, Murray Warmath from Humboldt, Tennessee, who had played from 1932 to 1934 and had been a Vol assistant coach (1936–39, 1946–49). He had also been Coach Robinson's collegiate roommate at Tennessee. It was another of those games that featured ex-Vols on opposing sidelines. On taking the Tennessee job in 1926, General Neyland had promised to make the Vol program "a cradle of coaches," and that promise was often fulfilled in the decades to follow. One of the State assistant coaches was former Vol end Denver Crawford, the captain of the 1947 Vol squad from Kingsport, Tennessee.

Based on the records of earlier seasons, the Gay Street odds makers had installed Tennessee as a "solid" seven-point favorite. Tennessee was ranked number 16 in *Look* magazine and number 17 in the Associated Press poll. Mack Franklin of Madisonville, an All-SEC selection at end a year earlier, was team captain. Tennessee was coming off an 8-2-1 record in 1952, so the top 20 ranking was likely based more on what the Vols had done a season earlier than what they might do in 1953. The Vols quickly fell from the rankings after the two season-opening losses and returned to the top 20 at number 18 before the Florida game on November 14. After a loss to Kentucky the next week, the Vols dropped from the top 20 and never returned that season.

The attendance that day was estimated at a "disappointing" 25,000, a far cry from the multitudes that flock to the much-bigger stadium on fall Saturdays these days. Media reports indicated that fans were having a hard time "warming up" to the beginning of the season.

John Majors, the pride of Huntland, Tennessee, was a freshman tailback, who, as Marvin West has noted, arrived on campus with little or no fanfare, despite being the Tennessee prep scoring leader for three consecutive years. Residents of the towns of Huntland (Franklin County) and Lynchburg (Moore County) often clash over Majors's hometown status, with both towns claiming him. "Lynchburg was my home until I was 15 years old," Majors wrote in his autobiography. The 2011 *University of Tennessee Media Guide* lists Majors's hometown as Huntland.

"When the 1950 season rolled around, I was a Huntland Hornet," Majors said. "We finally got an apartment for a few weeks, and then we moved into a frame house just a block from downtown, pretty much like our home in Lynchburg."[4] That statement would suggest that there was enough John Majors to go around between the two towns.

Tennessee head coach Bowden Wyatt with "1956 Stars" John Majors (left) and "Papa" John Gordy. U.T. Sports Information Office.

Kickoff was at 2 P.M. Local radio impresario George Mooney, who died in October 2011, was in his second year broadcasting Tennessee football, joined by local radio personality Art Metzler and spotter Julian Andes, a former Tennessee football manager. Former Vol All-America Bob Foxx (1938–40) would not arrive on the network until 1956.

Newspaper reports and advertisements in game programs indicated that the pre-game show, such as it was, began at 1:45 P.M. There was no post-game show, unless you count everyone's favorite, a call-in show called "Hold That Line." All of this took place on Knoxville's WROL Radio, later to be WATE, later WETE. Edwin Court Huster, Sr., headed up the fledgling network, after he and Lindsey Nelson had crisscrossed the state in the late 1940s garnering stations one-by-one.

The selection of the new mascot by the UT Pep Club was a big deal as a sidebar to the game, as noted by an *Orange and White* story, entitled "Man's Best Friend Gets Man's Toughest Job," two days earlier.

The football game tomorrow [*sic*] at Shields-Watkins Field may go down in U-T history for another reason besides the salient one that it marks the beginning of the coaching regime of Harvey Robinson. The student body will be introduced to its new mascot—a hound dog. For three years, the writer has listened to one gripe, bitch, and complaint after another against the lack of pep and genuine student interest at the football games. It does not seem excessively optimistic that a sad-eyed dog, more by the humor of his appearance than any connection to what the historians persist in calling "Tennessee's glorious past," might capture the interest of that better element of the student body which is not given over completely to a shallow sophomoric cynicism. The *Orange and White* believes, therefore, that the students should give the new arrival a break and meet him halfway.

The game took place in those halcyon days the Vols opened the last Saturday in September, played their ten games and went home, unless, of course, there was a bowl game. There were no open dates, or bye weeks, as they're known today.

The Tennessee media guide indicated that the squad numbered 46, with 27 returning letter winners. There had been 36 letter winners lost the past two seasons. The Vols lined up with captain Mack Franklin and Roger Rotroff, a senior from of Glendale, Ohio, at the ends. All-SEC selection Bob Fisher, a senior from Cleveland, Ohio, and Darris McCord, a junior from Franklin, Tennessee, an All-America selection and captain of the 1954 team and later a stalwart with the Detroit Lions, lined up at tackle. John Powell, a senior from Mt. Pleasant, Tennessee, and Bob Scott, a sophomore from Cleveland, Tennessee, were at the guards. Lamar Leachman, a junior from Cartersville, Georgia, was at center. Bill "Moose" Barbish, a senior from Cleveland, Ohio, was the blocking back. Jerry Hyde, a senior from Fort Wayne, Indiana, was the wingback. Ted Schwanger, a sophomore from Sandusky, Ohio, was the fullback, while Jimmy Wade, a junior from Lynchburg, Virginia, started at tailback.

The game was fought that afternoon, in the days long before ESPN Sports Center (before television on a large scale, really) and before the twenty-four-hour coverage of Tennessee sports. There weren't even "media timeouts" on the field in those days. The newspapers back then carried a complete hour-by-hour summary of the day's radio programs. Football in Big Orange Country was still big, but nothing like today.

Was that day memorable? Yes. It was a day the Tennessee Vols lost a game, the first season-opening loss since 1948, and gained a mascot.

The Mississippi State Maroons—they hadn't become Bulldogs yet—won 26–0 on that hot September afternoon, dominating play all day. Jackie Parker, a Tennessee youth who got away from Knoxville's Young High School, led the way for State, scoring twice, throwing a TD pass, kicking two extra points, making a number of tackles, and, just to cap his day off, booting the ball out of bounds at the Tennessee 2.

Underneath the south end zone, where the visitor's locker room was located, Mississippi State Coach Warmath was ecstatic. "Boys, you've made me the happiest coach in the United States. Here, I'll write it up on the blackboard."[5]

However, on the positive side from the Tennessee point of view, a canine named Brooks' Blue Smokey stole the show, and there has been a Smokey on the Vol sideline ever since.

No one knew how the hounds would react to the Shields-Watkins Field crowd and how the crowd would react to each dog. The Vols trailed State 13–0 at the half, giving rise to the thought that the crowd might not have been in

Knoxvillian Jackie Parker (12) from Young High School was the unquestioned star of the 1953 season opener. That is, unless you count the selection of Smokey I at halftime. Unfortunately for the Vols, Parker played for Mississippi State, and the Maroons won 26–0. Courtesy of Bud Fields.

the best humor anyway. On the other hand, anything that could distract the crowd's attention from the deficit might have been welcome. The university was committed to selecting a mascot, and the owners of each animal on display had to take their chances with the taste and whims of the Vol football public—it was a hound dog beauty pageant of the first order.

How many dogs were there to select from? No one is completely certain. Mildred Brooks had said there were 20, while a story in the *News Sentinel*, many years later on December 24, 1991, indicated there were 19. That came on the heels of the death of Smokey VI. "The number varies," Earl Hudson said. "I've heard 19, 9, and 4. It all depends on whom you ask."

Bart Pittman's *Knoxville Journal* story of September 27, 1953, indicates that some took a different, less sanguine, view of the proceedings. A city of

Knoxville humane officer present at the game had some official disdain and stuffiness present in his comments. "Better not be any holes in the fence where any of the mutts can get out," he said. "I'll run all four of them to City Pound if they get out. There's a quarantine on here now, you know." None of them got out, and the public welfare and health across the city avoided an onslaught of hounds.

Hal Ernest remembered that the contest took place, not at the Rose Hole, as initially advertised, but on the cheerleaders' ramp on the east side of Shields-Watkins Field. There would be a larger crowd at the game than at the Rose Hole, it was reasoned. The selection would be made based on the crowd reaction at the game.

"It was like a beauty pageant," Ernest, who had a public address microphone in hand as the dogs paraded across the ramp, remembered. "The dogs all looked alike. We paraded them out, with Smokey the last dog in line."

The "last one," he said, "was really excited. There was no question which dog was more animated. He was the obvious winner." Here's another perspective, from Reverend Brooks. "He was the last dog in the line," Reverend Brooks said. "When they came to him, they said, 'This is old Smokey.' The students were supposed to cheer for the dog they wanted."

And cheer they did.

"He barked. And they cheered for him. He barked again. He'd just throw his head back, and he had an awful voice anyway." There were rumors that Reverend Brooks might have prompted Blue Smokey to bark, but he denied the charge vehemently. "No, I didn't get him to bark. I wasn't standing near him when he was introduced. He just heard those cheers and got excited, but he had been in a lot of shows and was pretty well trained. He heard those cheers and got excited."

Earl Hudson termed the interaction between Blue Smokey and the crowd a "lovefest." There seemed to be no doubt that this dog had won a "bark-off" over at least three other dogs.

The mascot selection was not actually made official until the Duke game the next week, but every indication, including press reports from the game, hinted that "Brooks' Blue Smokey" was the obvious choice. *News Sentinel* cartoonist Bill Dyer inked a cartoon rendition of what appeared to be Smokey in tears at game's end as part of his famed DyerGram. "They picked a sad-eyed houn' dog for a mascot," Dyer wrote in his game commentary on September 27.

Smokey I with an earlier handler inspecting the east side of Shields-Watkins Field. U.T. Sports Information Office.

"He had a right to be!" (After the season-ending loss to Houston, 33–19, Siler also wrote that, "Even Smoky, the new blue tick hound mascot, shed a tear over that one.")[6]

In his September 27, 1953, *Knoxville Journal* story, Pittman also wrote that, as Worden has noted more than once, there was a lack of spirit at the game. "The crowd in general was very quiet and almost lacking in enthusiasm. The student cheering section, always the center of resounding yells in the past, failed to perform its usual job of sparking vigorous applause for the Vols." Reverend Brooks remembered how special the dog that would become Smokey I was. "That was a mighty good coon dog. I bought him four years ago at 11:30 in the woods near Chattanooga. He had just treed his second coon, and I told the others, 'I want that dog.' I had done a lot of hunting with him. He had won some dog shows. In fact I had turned down $500 for him—that was pretty good money in those days." That translates to more than $4,500 in 2009 dollars.

"Smokey I will always be number one to me," Reverend Brooks said in 1983. "He was the most sensible one. He was close to me because he was my personal coondog. We went hunting together. I never hunted with the others."[7]

Then came dealing with the details. How would the dog be cared for? That was, as we have seen, a major concern. "We had an offer in hand from W. C. Brooks which was very attractive," Worden said. "He wanted to provide a Bluetick Coonhound. His offer was irresistible. He would do everything. He would provide the dog, the housing, would have them at the games, would take care of all the feeding, and the lineage as long as his family could do it."

In a front page *Knoxville Journal* story the day after the Mississippi State game on September 27, Pittman led with a description of the scene at halftime as the hounds were presented. Then followed by a picture of the hounds with majorettes Betty Shelton, Faye Brown, Mary Lee Thomas, and Ann Thompson. "Four sad-faced hound dogs competing for mascot of the University of Tennessee Volunteers seemed less forlorn than many of the estimated 25,000 fans at Shields-Watkins Field yesterday, as the Mississippi State Maroons trampled Tennessee 26–0. In fact, the long-eared pooches appeared to draw louder yells when they were paraded before the student cheering section than the players in the gridiron battle on the turf. 'Blue Smokey,' owned by Reverend W. C. Brooks of Mascot, apparently was chosen over the other three dogs because of the roaring applause he received."

There was a later vote in the Pep Club, with the Brooks's Bluetick Coonhound the paws-down winner at the meeting. Stuart Worden was impressed with the possibilities. Everything seemed to be falling in place.

The logistics were the major element that made it possible. I never had the impression I was being sold. I had the impression he wanted very much to see his dog accepted. He made an offer for us no one else did. For a group of college students who didn't have the money or the contacts to make that happen, this looked extremely attractive.

We went out to see Reverend Brooks on Rutledge Pike. He showed us the dog and the kennels, the entire operation he had. It was obvious he was well equipped to back up his offer. He continued to do that through the years. That's where it happened.

The announcement of the dog's selection would be made the next week, but there was little doubt who the winner might be. Chambliss Pierce's prediction from September 24 was about to become reality. Dora Smith of the *Orange and White* also seemed to be prescient about the selection, writing on October 1, 1953, that "Although the winner's name was not announced, viewers had little doubt as to which pooch showed the most personality and received the most cheers." There were big plans for Smokey I at the Duke game on October 3, with Smith noting that "students sitting in the card trick section ... are asked to wear white shirts and rooter caps, have shakers, and stay seated at halftime."

Reverend Brooks did have a date with destiny, being notified by phone that Blue Smokey had won the contest. Could he bring Smokey to the Duke game the next Saturday, the caller queried?

"Bill was excited," Earl Hudson said. " He enjoyed being in the public eye."

"As far as I know, Bill and Mildred had never been to a Tennessee football game until that day," Y. C. Hudson said.

The *Orange and White* story quoted Stuart Worden, with the selection apparently in his back pocket, being optimistic about the prospects for the new mascot, saying, "The U-T mascot will rival that of any other school in the south."

The new Smokey made a grand entrance on the field at halftime of the Duke game, after having been awakened from a nap on the sidelines, walking along a white carpet, and thereby reflecting the way he behaved at the tryouts and what Mildred Brooks had said about him. "The first Smokey was a show dog. And he loved attention," she said. "I think they're a beautiful breed, just a little bit different from a lot of the breeds you see."

Wes Pritchard of Cleveland, Tennessee, a member of the Pep Club, and Dianne Darning of Knoxville, escorted the dog to the middle of the field, dressed, as was Reverend Brooks, in a "Li'l Abner" motif.

The announcement of the new mascot was the worst kept secret in town. Brooks' dog was the winner of the contest and, by nomination of Hubert Duncan of Kingsport, he would be called Smokey.

Ms. Ruth Ann Barker, the reigning "Miss Tennessee," placed a tailor-made orange-and-white jacket on Smokey. For his part, Smokey had a grand and glorious debut.

Smokey I was led to the field on a white carpet to receive the plaudits of the crowd at the 1953 Duke game. U.T. Photographic Services.

Local journalists had a field day with the new dog.

Ralph Griffith, *Knoxville Journal,* October 4, 1953: "Smoky walked out onto the field and allowed himself to be placed on a stand. He didn't even look for a tree or a fireplug one time." Ben Byrd, *Knoxville Journal,* October 4, 1953: "The sadness of the pageant extended to Tennessee's new mascot 'Smoky.' This pore old hound dog looked like he had lost his last friend. But if you didn't look at his ears you couldn't distinguish him from the parlay player who had the Vols and 10 points." Tom Anderson, the often-irreverent columnist of the *Knoxville Journal,* wrote this piece of doggerel on October 5:

> It might be a big honor,
> Mascoting this platoon
> But I'd rather be alone
> Chasing a coon.

Smokey being weighed somewhere on campus, 1953. From the numbers on the scale, Smokey I appears to weigh 90 pounds. U.T. Photographic Services.

Bob Wilson, sports editor of the *News Sentinel,* wrote that the selection of Smokey during halftime had another impact on the Duke game. "At the start of the third quarter, Tennessee was penalized 15 yards with Duke being allowed to kickoff from midfield. Gus Manning, U-T publicist, announced over the press box that the penalty was because the Vols had delayed the start of the third quarter by not having the field cleared of Ol' Smoky, the Vols' new hound dawg mascot, and majorettes in time to resume play after the regulation rest period."

For its part, the *Orange and White* praised the work of the Pep Club, and Worden specifically, in the history-making occurrence after Homecoming Day in the November 12 edition. "Tennessee has long needed a mascot and the frats utilized Ol' Smoky to the 7th degree in their displays, which, too, seemed to be very good in general," Sproul wrote. "Betty Cowart, Stu Worden, and Sammy Dennison—the main cogs in the wheel—and all their committees deserve a big clap on the back for a job well done."

The University of Tennessee thus had its mascot, a mascot from Mascot.

Smokey I with Ruth Ann Barker and Stuart Worden under the east stands of Shields-Watkins Field on September 26, 1953. Stuart Worden.

Rev. Bill Brooks welcomes Smokey II "home" after his kidnapping by University of Kentucky students at the 1955 Kentucky game at Stoll Field in Lexington, Kentucky. *Knoxville News Sentinel*.

Smokey III with Auburn head football coach Ralph (Shug) Jordan. U.T. Sports Information Office.

Smokey IV with handler Sam Huffaker of Knoxville on November 31, 1979. Smokey IV died December 4 that year. *Knoxville News Sentinel.*

Top: Smokey V and Uga, the Georgia bulldog mascot, before the 1980 Georgia game. Courtesy Sonny Seiler and Kent Hannon.

Bottom: Smokey VI on the artificial turf covering Shields-Watkins Field with his favorite team's helmet. Earl Hudson collection.

Smokey VII stands ever vigilant, watching his favorite team play. *University of Tennessee Sports Information Office.*

A happy looking Smokey VIII takes a break in Earl Hudson's front yard. Earl Hudson collection.

Smokey IX with his handlers and University of Tennessee cheerleaders at Bryant-Denny Stadium in Tuscaloosa, Alabama. U.T. Sports Information Office.

6

THE LEGACY OF
THE SMOKEYS

News Sentinel sports editor Tom Siler had pointedly asked the question in February 1955.[1]

Why have a mascot, particularly a hound dog?

Having a Smokey on the sidelines after nearly six decades proves that the mascot has had staying power, that commitments made in the early 1950s between a group of college students and a local minister could still be honored nearly sixty years later. Bill Brooks and his wife started it all. Then Earl Hudson and his wife took over. The question whether or not to have a mascot never had to be debated again.

As Reverend Brooks had promised Stuart Worden, he would take care of everything as far the Bluetick was concerned. That was a given to be honored and cherished, much like a church pledge or marriage vow. It's a commitment that has spanned the generations. "There were a lot of deals like that in the 1950s. There was nothing on paper," Worden recalled. "He said, 'You have my word.' That was good enough for us. He was pleased to have his dog selected. There was no money, no tickets. He never asked for it. He was so proud of his dog."

The dogs were born to the job, born to be the mascot. One by one the Smokeys were there, ready to go, when their number was called.

Smokey I (December 24, 1946–January 28, 1955) was the first. His official name was "PR Brooks Blue Smokey." His football seasons were 1953–54 under head coach Harvey Robinson. The teams he kept bayful watch over finished with a record of 10–10–1 (.500). These were rather lean times in the colorful

A very young pup who would become Smokey II in early 1955, shown with Stuart Worden. Courtesy of Stuart Worden.

history of Big Orange Country, so this dog was one of the really positive things to look forward to on a fall Saturday.

Smokey II (October 16, 1954–November 25, 1963) followed as the Smokey whose tenure was the most exciting. He was on the job from 1955 through the Kentucky game of 1963. His official name was "PR Brooks Blue Smokey II." He served under head coaches Bowden Wyatt and Jim McDonald. His overall record was 53–34–4 (.618). He was the first of the Smokeys to have a Tennessee football connection, being born on the day Tennessee lost to Alabama in 1954, 27–0 at Shields-Watkins Field.

Smokey III (June 18, 1964–1977), official name "PR Brooks Blue Smokey III," came on as mascot in 1964 and served until 1977, the longest tenure of any dog. He served during the Vols' resurgence of the mid-1960s, with 10 bowl games under his collar. He served under head coaches Doug Dickey, Bill Battle, and John Majors. He had a record of 109–44–6 (.704).

Smokey IV (September 24, 1973–December 4, 1979), also known as "PR Blue Smokey Joe," served in 1978 and 1979, with a record of 12–10–1 (.543). He

Smokey III with cheerleader Jeannie Gilbert and Adawayhi president Keith Richardson from May 1968. U.T. Photographic Services.

was born two days after the Vols had defeated Army 37–18 at Michie Stadium in West Point, New York. He served under Battle and Majors.

Smokey V (June 1, 1980–1984), official name "PR Brooks Blue Smokey V," was 28–18–1 (.606) during his tenure (the Vols had not defeated Alabama since 1970), serving through 1983. He was there for the streak-breaking win over Alabama in 1982, the first win for the Vols over Alabama since a 24–0 win in 1970 at Neyland Stadium. It was legendary Alabama Coach Paul (Bear) Bryant's last game in Neyland Stadium. Smokey VI was present and voting for another victory over the Tide a year later. He served under Majors.

Smokey VI (October 15, 1982–December 19, 1991), also known as "PR Brooks Blue Smokey VI," was born the day before the Alabama win. He served from 1984 to 1991 and was part of a 67–24–5 (.724) record, all under Majors. The Vols won three SEC titles during his reign (1985, 1990, 1991) and were involved in two of the greatest games in Tennessee history, the 1986 Sugar Bowl victory over Miami and the memorable comeback at Notre Dame in 1991.

Smokey VII, shown with two handlers, around 1992 or 1993. U.T. Photographic Services.

Smokey VII (August 29, 1991–1994) born as "PR Brooks Blue Smokey VII," was born less than two weeks before the Vols' season-opening game at Louisville. He served from 1992 to 1994, with a record of 27–9 (.750) under Majors and Phillip Fulmer.

Smokey VIII (September 14, 1994–March 17, 2006), born "PR Hudsons Blue Smokey VIII," was the national championship dog, serving from 1995 to 2003 with a record of 91–22 (.805). He was born three days before grass came back to Neyland Stadium in 1994. He also has two SEC titles under his collar, in 1997 and 1998. He served under Fulmer.

Smokey IX (September 5, 2003–present), christened "PR Hudson's Blue Smokey IX," was born the day before Tennessee defeated Marshall 34–24 in the season's second game. He has been on the job ever since, compiling a record of 67–47 (.587). He served under Fulmer, Lane Kiffin, and Derek Dooley.

Smokey VIII has obviously caught sight of something that made him happy. U.T. Photographic Services.

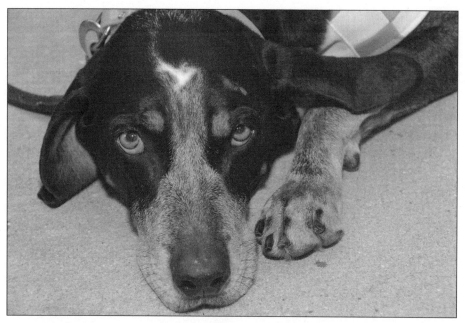

It's a brief moment of relaxation for Smokey IX in the midst of his hectic schedule. Courtesy of Jack Williams.

But apart from the statistics and these brief descriptions, the dogs have led exciting lives, the stuff of which legends are made.

Smokey I was a novelty on campus from the day he was selected. Harvey Sproul remembered how Tennessee students took to Smokey, writing in the *Orange and White* edition of November 12, 1953, as follows: "I had the dubious privilege of letting Ol' Smoky take me over to the game. (I mean this literally.) This is another good thing; it is really great how our new mascot has caught the fancy of the students and the general public." In a story written in the *Orange and White* on November 5, 1953, entitled "It's a Dog's Life, But Smokey's Not Complaining," the writer says that, "Smokey has always loved audiences, and he's really been eating up the attention he's been getting."

He was quite a charming dog. "When the photographer steps up with camera in hand, you'd swear Smokey smiles and strikes a special pose," said Ruth Ann Barker, the reigning Miss Tennessee. In the *Orange and White* of October 10, Shields Remine indicated that Smoky had distinguished company during his first year, writing just before the Chattanooga game that, "Smokey will again be present, with his pulchritudinous keeper, Miss Ruth Ann Barker.

Smokey I was killed on this deserted stretch of U. S. Highway 11W near Reverend Brooks's home on a Friday night in late January 1955. The picture looks to the south, where Smokey I was struck crossing the street by a northbound motorist. Tom Mattingly.

Stuart Worden, Pep Club head, said plans call for Smoky to smile and sing whenever Tennessee scores a win in future games, reserving his dour expression for sadder games."

But Smokey I received the most tribute after he was accidentally killed on Rutledge Pike, now Old Rutledge Pike, in East Knox County on a cold Friday night, January 28, 1955. The *Knoxville Journal* had the story in its January 30 issue.

> The dog got out of Reverend Brooks's garage and was hit just a few minutes later. "Smokey had never been kept in the lot and was never permitted to run loose," Reverend Brooks said. 'But because of the cold weather, we decided to put him in the garage. A stove provided warmth.
>
> That plan might have worked, but for one oversight. "A door was left unfastened. Smokey got outside, and the door closed. We missed him and started a search. We found him a few minutes after he had been hit by the car."

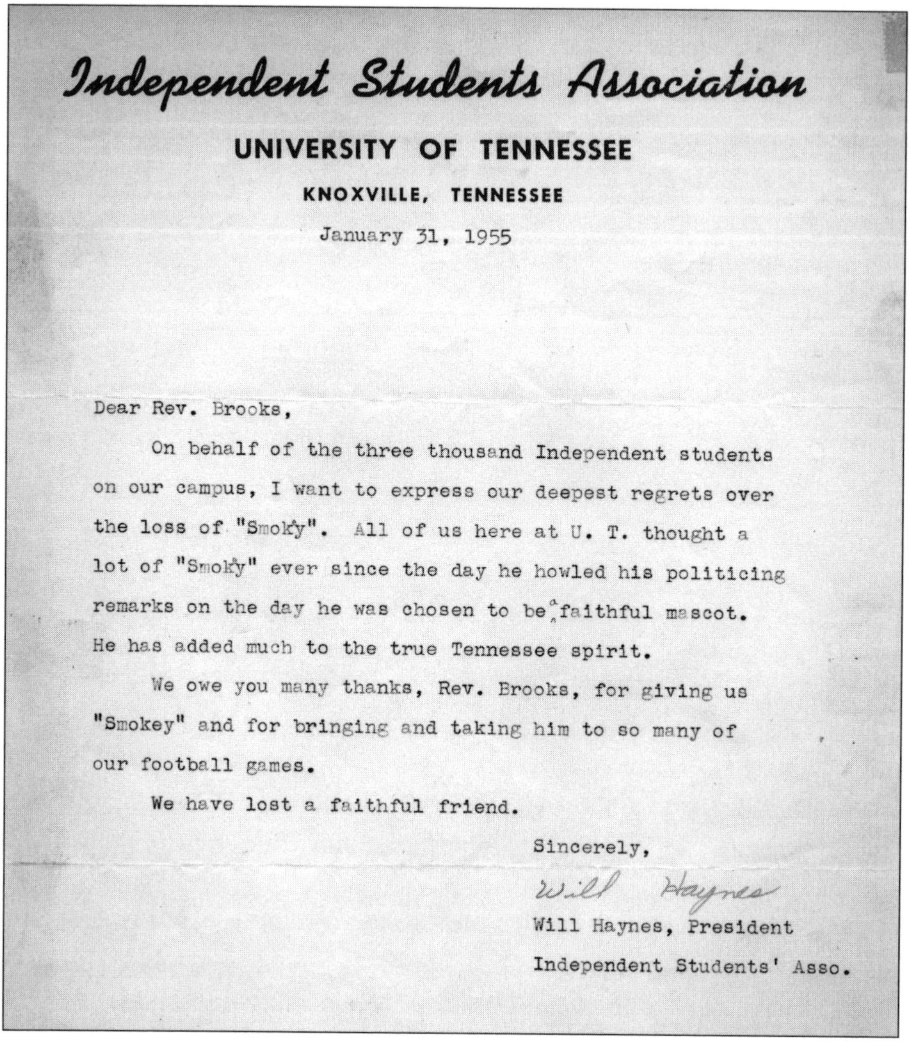

Independent Students Association

UNIVERSITY OF TENNESSEE
KNOXVILLE, TENNESSEE
January 31, 1955

Dear Rev. Brooks,

On behalf of the three thousand Independent students on our campus, I want to express our deepest regrets over the loss of "Smoky". All of us here at U. T. thought a lot of "Smoky" ever since the day he howled his politicing remarks on the day he was chosen to be faithful mascot. He has added much to the true Tennessee spirit.

We owe you many thanks, Rev. Brooks, for giving us "Smokey" and for bringing and taking him to so many of our football games.

We have lost a faithful friend.

Sincerely,

Will Haynes

Will Haynes, President
Independent Students' Asso.

Will Haynes, president of the Independent Students Association, sent a letter expressing sympathy for the death of Smokey I. Earl Hudson collection.

The story went on to say that "the driver of the car stopped, reversed his car to the spot where Smoky was struck, and then sped away." Always looking ahead, Reverend Brooks added, "Smokey has four sons who will make good mascots."

Photos in the *Journal* showed Reverend Brooks and friends Ray Mink and Leon Bozeman burying Smokey I at the Brooks home just off Rutledge Pike. Smokey I's death stunned the campus, breaking the tranquility. "We owe you many thanks, Rev. Brooks, for giving us 'Smokey' and for bringing him and taking him to so many of our football games," Will Haynes, president of the Independent Students Association, wrote in a January 31, 1955, letter. "We have lost a faithful friend. He has added much to the Tennessee spirit." That same day, head cheerleader Wawanna Cameron, now Wawanna Widoff, wrote that "I feel as this is a great loss to the entire university, as well as to you all. I am leaving the university this year, but I would like to tell you how I have enjoyed knowing you all and also 'Smoky.'"

Gordon Goodgame, now Rev. Gordon Goodgame, retired from the United Methodist Church, remembered the good times with the Brooks family and with Smokey. He had quite a career at Tennessee, starting as a cheerleader. "My cheerleading came to an end after the 1952 season with a political coup," he said. "I was Pep Club President in 1954 and Pep Coordinator (Student Council Office) in 1955."

That led him to a friendship with Bill and Mildred Brooks. "I kept Smokey when Reverend Brooks could not make it to the games. On occasion, I kept him at the Sigma Phi Epsilon fraternity house (he liked to party) or took him home with me to Lincoln Park," Reverend Goodgame said. "It was all very informal in those days, even though the novelty was growing. Smokey stayed out at the farm (which also housed Bill's Clutch Shop, Reverend Brooks's primary employment) on Rutledge Pike."

With Smokey I deceased, another dog needed to be found . . . and quickly.

Reverend Goodgame remembered helping look for a Smokey II who would be a direct descendant and look and act as much like Smokey I as possible. The *Orange and White* reported on September 22, 1955, that there would be a new Smokey on duty when the Vols squared off against Mississippi State at Shields-Watkins Field. The game would also be Bowden Wyatt's debut as Tennessee head coach. The Vols lost that one, 13–7, but better days were ahead for Bowden . . . and for Smokey II, described in the *Orange and White* as a "chip off the old block."

A TRIBUTE FROM SMOKEY II TO HIS DAD SMOKEY I

EDITOR'S NOTE: The following was turned into the *Orange and White* scrawled on discarded dog biscuit.

This is what you might call the end of an era, a time of bountiful change and prosperity. From each change in the dial of history a figurehead arises to hover over and affect the lives of myriads of we miserables. Yet this is a tale of a figurehead among figureheads, my father Smoky.

From the first day I could remember thumping my tail, I knew I had been born into something great and magnificent. But little did I realize the honor with which my heritage had endowed me. Not content with being a mere hound-dog, my father had earned the noble distinction" Blue Tick Coon Hound." We were not only blue bloods, ours had that deep indigo tint.

Early in my days, I frollicked not, but learned to bear myself according to my station in life. I carefully and methodically imitated my father's every movement—the way he drug his ears in the dust, the silent solitude in his mournful howl, the bearing of his prominent nose always so cold and wet.

The years fled by, and dad received pedigree upon pedigree from the four corners of the earth. There were diamond studded muzzles from Farouk's collies, ermine mufflers from Ali Khan pekenese [sic], but they were far overcome by what was to come.

Early on bright Saturday morning, a smooth talking young man [Stuart Worden, perhaps?] came to take to Rev. Brooks (our owner) and asked for his permission to use my sire as official mascot of the University of Tennessee. Little prickles of priceless ecstasy stole along my fur, and my pride was without bounds.

The infinite achievements of Smokey as official mascot are common knowledge: the time he bit Bobby Dodd, the fleas he gave to Florida's alligator, and his pleasant odor the fans always loved. There was always a pat from Donna or a hug from Barbara—ample reward for a job well done.

Yet as the years drug on, a change gradually crept over my idol: his hair thinned, his slouch grew, his growl grew mild, but the years never dimmed the sparkle in his eyes.

Suddenly, on that ill-fated night on Jan. 28, disaster struck. The football season was long forgotten, and Smokey along with it. The coon season was on, but hunters disagreed with his gout. A dejected dog was slowly crossing the road when a dastardly demon speeding through the night took the life of that sad-eyed rascal.

PAX VOBISCUM

The condolences pour in: a tombstone sponsored by the Pep Club will be erected, a life sized picture of dad will be hung in the Hall of Fame at the Student Center entitled "Smokey I," and letters of sympathy pour in from friends across the earth.

His successor will have a great deal to live up to. Maybe me.

(This story, from the February 3, 1955, edition of the *Orange and White,* carried the byline of Bill Newman, identified in the 1955–56 *Volunteer* yearbook as the art editor of the publication. That dog did, in fact, become Smokey II, a dog that was part of the memorable moments in the lineage of the Smokeys.)

The story mentioned a "new howl" arising from the stands, "a new howl indeed, yet eerily reminiscent of an ever-depressed, much loved friend." The story went on to say that the ten-month-old pup "will remind many upperclassmen of the sparkling, yet sad eyes, the drooping tail, the hanging jowls, and the curling ears of his late father—the original Smokey." Reverend Brooks had picked Smokey's successor, the story said, from among fourteen of his sons scattered throughout the United States. "Their choice has a seven generation pedigree backing up his blue blood," the story stated. "Translated, this means 241 ancestors on the record—the finest pedigree available."

The story concluded with a warning to the "fair damsels" among the readers. (You couldn't write that type copy these days.) In an eloquent statement, among many flowery pieces of prose in the text, there was a word of caution: "If you feel a wet nose on your leg, don't shriek, for its more than likely a rather discouraged hound stripped from the companionship of female cheerleaders."

Smokey II had a glorious career, complete with all kinds of magic moments. "He had a real fine history," said Hudson.

In his rookie season, University of Kentucky students dognapped him before the game at Lexington. Things were hot and heavy in the rivalry back then, and the mascots of both schools were involved in the contretemps. It started with a Kentucky law student named Beauchamp Brogan, who had graduated from Tennessee. He was a Delta Tau Delta member at Kentucky, just as he had been in Knoxville.

"In the week before the game," he recalled in a story in the *Knoxville Journal* on November 22, 1985, "several of us were talking about doing something to stir things up." The plan, he said, was to steal Smokey. Brogan was perfectly situated to pull off the caper, having been a U.T. student, having been president of the Pep Club, and, most importantly, having a Tennessee license plates on his car.

Mildred Brooks picks up the story. "These boys came over to the house and said they were with the Pep Club and they were supposed to take Smokey for some pictures. We checked them out. They had Tennessee plates on their car and seemed to know us." Reverend Brooks even remembered one other aspect of the dognapping. "They even had me pretending like I was saying good-bye to him," he said. Red flags went up, Mrs. Brooks said, when, "Smokey was not returned to us by noon. We knew something was wrong."[2]

Brogan and crew hightailed it to Middlesboro, and Brooks later received a postcard (two cents postage affixed), addressed to "Rev. Willie Brooks, Rutledge Pike, Knoxville, Tennessee," with a Corbin, Kentucky, postmark,

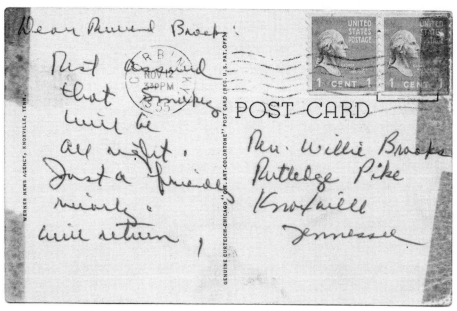

The postcard from "Blue Smoky's" captors to Reverend Brooks explaining the rationale behind the "dognapping." Earl Hudson collection.

dated November 12 at 3:30 P.M. "Rest assured Smokey will be all right. Just a friendly rivalry. Will return."

According to press reports, Brogan and crew took Smokey to a Lexington horse farm, giving the owner instructions on how to care for the dog, saying that Smokey "was treated like a king." Then they called the local media to "let everyone know Smokey was alive and well."

Tennessee students responded to the dognapping. One group was apprehended—later released—after painting a large "UT" on Memorial Coliseum in Lexington. There was no word how legendary Kentucky basketball coach Adolph Rupp might have reacted to that turn of events. It couldn't have been good.

After that, the *Journal* story noted, Tennessee students, led by Gene Burton, catnapped a stuffed mascot named Kernel. The real Kernel, "the last living UK mascot, has been dead for two years and was still fresh in memory."

The whole affair became a scene of media frenzy that sent Knoxville reporters into full investigative mode, including the two *News Sentinel* photographers who finally chased down the story. "Mickey Creager and I knew Smokey had been dognapped when we went to Lexington the day before the game," remembered Bill Dye, a retired *Knoxville News Sentinel* photographer, just before he died in 2009. "We went to the Sports Publicity Office where they told us where we could find Smokey. The fraternity sent a crew over to pick us up. They blindfolded us and put us in the car. I didn't know anything about Lexington. I remember telling them that, 'One of us had to take the picture.'"

Bill related, "We went and saw Smokey and took the pictures, one of Smokey and one of Mickey Creager blindfolded. They took us back to the fraternity house, and we transmitted the pictures to Knoxville." Sportswriter Red Bailes reported in the *Knoxville News Sentinel* of November 19 that the photographers didn't know where they had found Smokey II, who was referred to as "Old Smoky II" in this story and in an accompanying story by Sports Editor Bob Wilson. Bailes added that Dye and Creager had been driven around Lexington for "20 minutes or so," while "changing cars a couple of times." He also mentioned that Smokey had looked "nervous" during the whole ordeal.

Smokey II, "dressed in a blue and white blanket with a large 'K,'" according to Bailes's *Knoxville News Sentinel* November 19, 1955, story, was present at a Kentucky pep rally the night before the game at Memorial Coliseum, an event that attracted a crowd of 5,000 students and Wildcat supporters. "We have had a rough time keeping the dog away from the hands of Kentucky boys who wanted to shave a 'K' on him," one of the captors was quoted as saying. "We have taken good care of the dog, and he'll be returned in excellent condition."

The exchange was made just before kickoff, after Smokey had spent "eight hectic days" in Lexington. Earl Hudson remembered that when Smokey was returned to the Tennessee side of the field at Stoll Field on game day Bill Brooks was at the ready with a steak for Smokey II, saying, "Welcome home."

That story was on page 1 in the *News Sentinel* that day. This "home edition" was likely delivered to subscribers and on the stands about the time the game was in progress or perhaps about the time the game was over.

According to the *News Sentinel* story, U.T. Dean of Students Dr. Ralph Dunford helped arrange a truce for the return of the mascots with University of Kentucky Dean of Men Dr. Leslie Martin. "We hope this will put an end to the whole episode, which was largely a publicity stunt engineered by a few students," Dunford said.

Today's Tennessee fans might be shocked to realize that Kentucky won 23–0 that day. Kentucky had thus won three in a row over the Vols and would not lose to the Vols the remainder of the decade, save for a 20–7 Vol win in Knoxville the next season.

For his part, Brogan later became the University of Tennessee's general counsel and chief legal officer in 1975 after a stint at TVA. According to a *Knoxville Journal* story from November 22, 1985, when he interviewed for the job, he questioned whether to tell the trustees about the Smokey saga. When he did, found support from Trustee Col. Tom Elam. "If he's smart enough to do that," Colonel Elam is reported to have said, "we ought to go ahead and hire him."

Then came another misadventure with Smokey II, as Vanderbilt students tried to get in on the act. "A week later after Kentucky returned Smokey II, Vanderbilt decided they would do the same thing," Earl said. "They went in and got a dog, but got the wrong one. They stole a hunting dog named Ol' Rusty." Mildred Brooks remembered "three embarrassed Vandy coeds who came to the house in the middle of the night to return the dog." Reverend Brooks and Mildred took great delight in this failed rescue attempt.

Smokey II was also the beneficiary of what passed for poetry in his honor following his release from captivity in Kentucky. In a column called "Assignment U-T, and Curt Mathis" the *Orange and White* of November 18 printed this doggerel, to be sung to the tune of "On Top of Old Smoky":

> U-K came for old Smoky,
> and took him away,
> but we'll get him back
> on this Saturday.
> In retaliation
> for our trick last year
> when we stole the keg—
> but minus the beer.
> Now listen you Wildcats,
> and take this to heed,
> you won't be forgiven
> for this unkind deed.
> At home Smok's a hero,
> we worship his mug.
> The Vols even bought him
> a golden fire plug.

As if getting stolen wasn't bad enough, Smokey II got crossways with the Baylor Bear, a bruin named Judge, at the 1957 Sugar Bowl.

"We warned the boys that that were taking Smokey down there to be careful of the Baylor Bear—he was a real live one—because we knew Smokey would want to go after him," Mildred Brooks said. "The bear did take a few swats at Smokey, but they were separated before any real harm could be done."

At the risk of exaggeration, one history of this confrontation between the two mascots, written from a Baylor point of view, takes an intriguing turn. "The 1957 Sugar Bowl is remembered for Baylor's upset of mighty Tennessee. But, it may best be remembered for an altercation between the two teams' animal mascots. On the sideline, Smokey II, Tennessee's hound dog mascot, mixed it up with the Baylor Bear." According to the same article, "There have been eight Smokeys since 1953, and all have lived happy, productive Houn' Dog lives (except for Smokey II, who was mauled by the Baylor Bear at the

Sugar Bowl in 1957. Smokey II wasn't himself afterwards, and the Baylor Bear was always a little bit more frisky."[3] There's no evidence any of this is true, at least on Smokey's side.

He remained the mascot for six more years, being featured in a 1957 band show, as Klein reported, where, in a light-hearted moment, "there was an Elvis tribute with an imitator singing, 'You Ain't Nothing but a Hound Dog.'"[4] But there were sad events, too. Under Smokey II's reign, legendary coach Gen. Robert Neyland passed away on March 28, 1962, at the Oschner Clinic in New Orleans.

If that wasn't bad enough, on November 23, 1963, a return visit to Kentucky took a tragic turn. It was the day after President Kennedy had been assassinated in Dallas. Smokey II died after someone, no one knows who or why, fed him a chocolate pie after the game at Stoll Field. Vets will tell you that chocolate is one of the worst things anybody could feed a dog. "It appeared to be whole chocolate pie, crust and everything. It was right there on the sidelines," Earl Hudson said. "Bill had Smokey on the leash. We didn't have a clue."

In an Associated Press report on Monday, November 25, an unnamed veterinarian said "acute indigestion" caused Smokey II's death on Sunday, November 24. "We were there in Lexington when he died," Earl said. "There was no way we would bring him back to Knoxville in an unconscious condition. Chocolate is very bad for dogs. Their digestive system can't tolerate chocolate. We took him to the vet. I understood he died the same day. It might have been that night, maybe after midnight."

Dr. Klein called it a "natural death," as did Steve Fielder in a May 1987 issue of *Coonhound Bloodlines*. "We didn't make a big deal about it," Earl Hudson said. "It had to be an innocent thing."[5]

Despite the tragedy, never fear. Reverend Brooks had a plan. "We did have a replacement ready. Bob Woodruff loaned us a dog for the Vanderbilt game the next week." At that time, Woodruff was interim athletics director, coming on board after Bowden Wyatt had been dismissed in June 1963. He would be named athletic director after the Vanderbilt game, in lengthy and contentious athletics board meetings the morning before and the evening after the game against the Commodores.

His first duty after being named A.D. was to recommend a new head football coach. His choice was Douglas Adair Dickey, an assistant coach under

This editorial cartoon, by the Knoxville Journal's Charlie Daniel, appeared the day after the death of General R. R. Neyland.

"GREAT GAME, COACH"

Charlie Daniel's devotion to U.T. football is shown in this tribute to General Neyland that appeared in the Knoxville Journal on March 29, 1962.

Frank Broyles at Arkansas, who had been Woodruff's quarterback at Florida in the early 1950s. Woodruff's son Joe, now living in Knoxville, remembered Blueticks being in the backyard of their home in West Knoxville. "I think we had several of them," he said. "He loved them. He didn't raise them or anything like that. There might have been two or three dogs," Joe said. That is, he said, until my mother "got fed up with the noise and demanded fewer dogs."

Smokey III didn't have a problem with a real bear as Smokey II had, but he did have a memorable conflict with an Alabama head coach known popularly as Bear Bryant, real name Paul William Bryant of Moro Bottom, Arkansas, and his sophomore quarterback, Scott Hunter.

The date was October 19, 1968, at Neyland Stadium. Tennessee was ranked number 8, while Alabama was unranked, at least by the Associated Press. The game was telecast nationally by ABC-TV, the only game on TV that weekend.

"We were warming up before the game and one of their cheerleaders kept letting Smokey, their mascot, come over close to us and bark," said Hunter. "I got tired of it and took a kick at that old hound." That was a bad move on his part. "Coach Bryant walked up beside me and said, 'Scott, we've got enough trouble up here without you trying to kick their dog.'" [6]

Smokey, along with other Vol fans, enjoyed a series of "Alabama jokes" in a Daniel cartoon for the *Knoxville Journal*. The Tennessee player doesn't seem to be laughing, having to actually line up against the Tide that day, but the Vols prevailed 10–9 on October 19, 1968.

Bryant was correct in his assessment of the 1968 game. Tennessee won 10–9 that day, as Jimmy Weatherford blocked a last-second Alabama field goal to make the entirety of Big Orange Country happy. It was the second victory over Alabama in as many years.

Smokey IV suffered from a definite case of stage fright, apparently due mainly to a reaction from the noise of exploding fireworks at a pep rally. "Tennessee crowds are loud and when the level of noise reached a peak," Fielder wrote, "Smokey IV had a tough time dealing with it."

Smokey IV was kept at UT. "Someone in authority at Tennessee indicated a desire to have Smokey be on campus, but it didn't work. He needed more care and protection." During his tenure, the AGR fraternity took over handling the succeeding Smokeys for special events. According to Smokey handler Al Williams who was with the dog (calling him a "shy creature") in the 1977 and 1978 seasons, Smokey IV was "quite the icon" on campus and was "always anxious to run through the 'T.' He was like a steam engine," Williams said,

Majorette Becky Nanney gets some quality time with Smokey III in a picture from the *Knoxville Journal*, November 1, 1968.

"always pulling. It took two of us to hold him on the way. When we said, 'Let's go,' he was ready."

Smokey IV died in December 1979 after a "valiant fight" with cancer, just before he was slated to go to Houston for the Astro-Bluebonnet Bowl game with Purdue. "With no offspring, the bloodline was broken," Klein wrote in an article in a campus newsletter entitled *Context* on October 10, 1991.

Here's Fielder's take on the death of Smokey IV. "When Smokey IV died, an unfortunate death of a dog in the family line forced Brooks to look elsewhere for a replacement, thus breaking the bloodline of the original mascot, Smokey." But with necessity being the mother of invention, Klein reported that "A Smokey look-alike was found through an ad in the *Knoxville Journal*."

Smokey V served from 1980 to 1983 and, in Hudson's words, was a "good one, one that looked like Smokey VIII." He became the mascot for the Georgia game to open the 1980 season at the tender age of twelve months. Jimmy Burton, his handler, remembered that "His ears dragged the ground. That's how little he was."

That was one nervous dog, Burton recalled. "I remember poor, little Smokey just shook like everything at the first couple of games. We couldn't get him to run through the T, either." There was a happy end to the story. "But it wasn't long before the pup had the hang of things and went on to enthusiastically lead the Vol spirit."

Smokey V and UGA got to know each other before the 1980 Georgia game in Knoxville. Courtesy of Sonny Seiler and Kent Hannon.

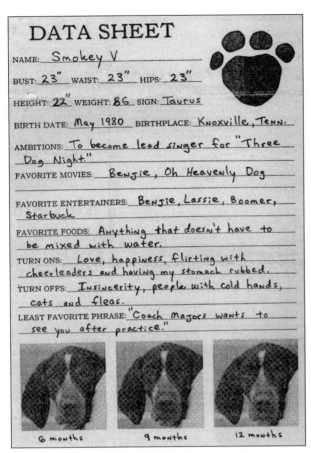

DATA SHEET

NAME: Smokey V

BUST: 23" WAIST: 23" HIPS: 23"

HEIGHT: 22" WEIGHT: 86 SIGN: Taurus

BIRTH DATE: May 1980 BIRTHPLACE: Knoxville, Tenn.

AMBITIONS: To become lead singer for "Three Dog Night."

FAVORITE MOVIES: Benjie, Oh Heavenly Dog

FAVORITE ENTERTAINERS: Benjie, Lassie, Boomer, Starbuck

FAVORITE FOODS: Anything that doesn't have to be mixed with water.

TURN ONS: Love, happiness, flirting with cheerleaders and having my stomach rubbed.

TURN OFFS: Insincerity, people with cold hands, cats and fleas.

LEAST FAVORITE PHRASE: "Coach Majors wants to see you after practice."

6 months   9 months   12 months

Smokey V was honored as one of the "Dogs of the SEC" in 1981. The dossier appeared in the *Knoxville Journal* on September 1.

Early in his career, he went nose-to-nose with Georgia's Uga and came out unscathed. "He stood off the Georgia Bulldog," Earl Hudson remembered, but didn't remember the exact game. The two teams played in Knoxville in 1980 and in Athens in 1981, both Georgia wins. "The handlers took him over to see Uga just to add some color and excitement, and they each showed a little attitude. It was nothing aggressive on their part, just like normal dogs do." Earl said it was a matter of boys being boys. "He gets along with all types of dogs, but you can't provoke him."

There was one problem with Smokey V that Reverend Brooks and Earl Hudson each identified. "He couldn't seem to stop growing. My wife made five jackets for him in a single season," Reverend Brooks said.

The *Knoxville Journal* ran a series called "Dogs of the Southeastern Conference," featuring Smokey V, in a spoof of a similar feature in *Playboy* magazine.

Bill and Mildred Brooks in the 1980s. Earl Hudson collection.

The profile in the September 4, 1981, issue noted that his measurements were 23 inches by 23 inches by 23 inches, his ambition was to be "Lead Singer for 'Three Dog Night,'" his favorite food was "Anything that doesn't have to be mixed with water," and his least favorite phrase was "Coach Majors wants to see you after practice."

Smokey V died in the summer of 1984, after being hit by a car.

Two years later, during the reign of Smokey VI, Reverend Brooks died on September 17, at age 75. During a lifetime of singular achievement, one of his proudest memories was taking care of these six fine mascots over thirty years, day in and day out.

"Bill wasn't sick very long," Earl Hudson recalled. "He was still active in the summer of 1986. He went pretty fast." Mildred Brooks took over responsibility for Smokey VI's care, aided by friends and neighbors, most notably Reverend Guy Milam and his son-in-law Charley Phelps.

Smokey VI was in on three SEC titles from 1984 to 1991. He was another of the decorated Smokeys and quite a survivor. The dog went down due to a heat stroke in the UCLA game that season, a contest played on artificial turf in oppressive September heat that affected players, fans, and mascots alike. The official temperature was 106 degrees, with television network WTBS reporting that temperatures were even higher on the field.

He missed the Mississippi State game the next week, and the University of Tennessee Sports Information Office was deluged by queries about his condition. He was also listed on the official injury report during that season. USA Today chronicled Smokey's condition on Monday, September 16, 1991, reporting that Smokey VI "was taken to the vet with breathing trouble after the Volunteers' 30–16 victory against UCLA." According to Earl Hudson, he was given "intravenous fluids, a cold water bath, and was treated for shock."

He remained on injured reserved until later in the season, when he recovered and returned to his duties, leading the Vols onto the field, howling all the way.[7]

Sometime in early November that season, Smokey VI was admitted to the hospital with a number of cancer-related symptoms. Dr. Robert DeNovo, associate professor of medicine at the University of Tennessee Veterinary Teaching Hospital, said the "type and location of the tumor prevented specialists from operating or using radiation or chemotherapy to halt its growth. He was sort of depressed and wasn't himself," Dr. DeNovo said. "He wasn't alert. He wasn't as perky. His appetite dropped off, and he started losing weight." He passed away on December 19, 1991.

"Mildred was starting to get sick about then, when Smokey VI died," Earl Hudson said. "She really didn't know where to go to get another Smokey, and some neighbors helped her find him." There were times during this period between Bill and Mildred's deaths that Smokey was living on a farm in Sevier County, but that arrangement had its pitfalls.

"In 1993, Mildred was apprehensive about Smokey VI's care and decided to bring him home," Hudson said. "That's where I came in. It was a matter of a brother helping his sister." As Mildred's health worsened, Earl finally took over caring for Smokey VII fulltime in 1994. Mildred died in 1997, due, as Earl said, "to the multiple problems of aging."

Smokey VII, who served from 1992 to 1994, has been called the "black sheep" of the line. He was replaced in the fall of 1994 after nipping at the heels of a band member, a tuba player named Tommy Chase, when the Vols ran through the "T" before a game. It didn't happen just once. It happened in consecutive games.

"That fellow had obviously stepped on his foot. Nobody ever explained that in the paper," Earl Hudson said. That was it for Smokey VII. He was replaced the remainder of the season by a dog named "Woody," who also belonged to former athletic director Bob Woodruff.

Smokey VIII started service in 1995 and has two SEC titles and a national championship under his collar. He retired after the 2003 season, making a final appearance at the Peach Bowl. His reign was second only to Smoky III's fourteen-year stand from 1963 to 1977.

Given all the comments about Smokey VIII, you'd have to conclude that he was a "damn good dog," as the Georgia folks have always said about Uga. "We didn't have to worry about him," Earl Hudson said. "He's been good to young and old people alike, babies even. He's always been active and never seems to tire of the attention."

Smokey VIII retired before the January 2, 2004, Peach Bowl game against Clemson. U.T. Photographic Services.

An aging Smokey VIII was on the sideline for the Peach Bowl, but did not run onto the field with his handlers. He did ride a float in the pregame parade.

He was diagnosed with a nasal tumor in December 2003, according to a Sports Information Office media release. "Smokey VIII responded very well to radiation treatment and chemotherapy for his nasal adenocarcinoma, surviving a year beyond his expected prognosis," Dr. Kate Stenske, Smokey's vet at the University of Tennessee Veterinary Hospital, said.

Earl Hudson remembered the magic moments, terming him "the best one we ever had. My relationship with Smokey VIII was special. I got him when he was two months old. He served with distinction, weathered storms, cold and heat. He came through it all real well and was always raring to go. He was a great mascot."

Smokey VIII did fall short in one area, obedience. As related by Tom Poste, in one memorable case, "It almost kept him from his duties at the 1998 Fiesta Bowl where his teammates won the national championship. He seemed out of sorts earlier and a trip to a local vet showed an obstruction in his colon. He'd scarfed down one of the hotel washcloths. The vet gave him the go ahead to appear at the game and wait until he got home to have the obstruction removed. Smokey charged onto the field and howled, bayed and belled his way through the game like nothing was wrong, then made it home and had the washcloth removed from his gut."[8]

Earl Hudson echoed Poste's comments. "We don't do a lot of obedience," Earl said at the time. "It's not in his repertoire." After a wonderful, long life, Smokey VIII died March 17, 2006, in Knoxville, the official cause of death being "complications from high blood pressure and kidney disease."

Earl remembered that when he went to look for Smokey IX, owner Jim Hackworth of Goose Creek, South Carolina, wanted three hundred dollars for the new dog. Too much money, Earl Hudson thought. Then Earl had an epiphany that cinched the deal. He told Hackworth that the dog would become Smokey IX. That settled that. Hackworth knocked a hundred bucks off the price.

This is a dog that also seemed to be ready to get to the games on a moment's notice. "He gets excited when the handlers come," Earl said.

When it came time for Smokey IX's debut at the 2004 UNLV game on September 5, handler Scott Walker said things might have been "iffy" at first. "He was a little taken aback by running through the 'T' the first time," Walker

Smokey IX takes a snooze on the grass of Shields-Watkins Field. U.T. Photographic Services.

said. "He is used to being around small groups of people, and then you throw him in there with 107,000 people running through the T with the football team behind him, he was really nervous. We had to help him along a little bit, but he did O.K."

Walker also noted the differences he saw between Smokey VIII and Smokey IX. "You have a whole other world in comparison. You have Smokey VIII who was an icon for nine seasons as he would stand at attention, pose for every picture, and he would run perfectly. The thing about Smokey IX is that he does have that puppy spirit. So he is more playful with the fans. He licks on them, nudges them around, and is just a lot more playful. But he is very friendly, and I think he is going to work out very well."

After taking over, Smokey IX caused a firestorm of controversy when it was alleged that he had nipped at, perhaps even bitten, an Alabama player during warm-ups before the 2006 game in Knoxville. Considerable back-and-forth followed between the Tennessee and Alabama sides. Alabama head coach Mike Shula said afterwards, "I can't confirm that. I wasn't an eyewitness, but I did see that it drew blood in pregame warm-ups." There was also considerable

An Uga substitute named Russ goes nose-to-nose with Smokey IX, who has also been accused of going after an Alabama player. These dogs always seem to mix it up. Courtesy of Sonny Seiler and Kent Hannon.

chatter among Alabama representatives outside the dressing room about what might have taken place. No one seemed happy.

As for Smokey IX, he wasn't injured and likewise wasn't available for comment. His predecessor had, however, addressed the matter of biting years earlier in a 1999 "interview" with Bill Traughber of *Big Orange Illustrated,* saying, "There have been times I have growled and snarled, but I have never bitten anyone. . . . The UT administration would consider that unprofessional for me."

Earl Hudson defended the honor of Tennessee's mascot. "Smokey did not bite him. The article in the paper said he bit the player. He got a little of his uniform, didn't break the skin I was told, but Alabama made a big deal out of it I understand," Earl Hudson said.

But there were also two happenings in 2009 and 2010 that caught the eye of Smokey fanciers everywhere. The first came on November 25, 2009, from the American Kennel Club. "The AKC this month made blue-tick hounds—like Smokey IX, the University of Tennessee mascot—the 162nd registered breed, meaning they are eligible to participate in sanctioned shows as of December

30," Robert Wilson wrote in the *Knoxville News Sentinel*. Wilson noted that "Blueticks are a lot like the folks of East Tennessee. They are friendly, loyal, resourceful and don't have much use for Florida Gators."

Then came another significant announcement on February 16, 2010, report from the Associated Press that appeared on the website Huffington Post that had to have gladdened the hearts of Smokey admirers everywhere. "Westminster will welcome six more breeds next year," a statement read, "including the bluetick coonhound, best known to sports fans as the Smokey mascot at the University of Tennessee."[9] But there was one note of caution, that the Blueticks would need a year to sort things out. "The bluetick is a 'redshirt freshman' and needs a year to qualify in local competitions," Westminster host David Frei said.

In February 2011, Smokey IX was again thrust into prominence when media reports (as well as the actual "confession" on the Paul Finebaum radio show) revealed that trees at "Toomer's Corner" in downtown Auburn, Alabama, had been poisoned, allegedly by a man named Harvey Updyke. Knoxville radio station WNML's Heather Harrington, a former Lady Vol athlete and a regular on the station's morning sports talk show, opined that the tree-poisoning incident was the equivalent to "poisoning Smokey." That might have been a bit over the top, but reveals the depth of passion fans have for their school and the symbols that help define it.

Not too many months after the tree poisoning at Auburn, in the fall of 2011, Smokey IX suffered the first of two prominent knee injuries involving the Vol football program. In the second quarter of the Cincinnati game on September 10, Dr. Darryl Millis, professor of orthopedic surgery from the University of Tennessee College of Veterinary Medicine noticed something wrong with the dog. He told a colleague that Smokey limped noticeably when he ran across the south end zone after a Tennessee touchdown, not appearing to be his usual self. A week later, Vol wide receiver Justin Hunter banged up a knee early in the Florida game and was lost for the season.

When word got out that Smokey IX was injured, the *News Sentinel* and the utsports.com website treated his injury with the attention that might have been devoted to a Tennessee player critical to the team's fortunes.[10] Maybe Smokey got more attention. Here's the *News Sentinel*'s version of Smokey IX's prognosis. "Since his ailment was diagnosed," John Adams wrote on September 26, 2011, "Smokey has been injected with platelet-rich plasma,

Smokey IX takes a sniff at the "Human Smokey." U.T. Photographic Services.

received electrical stimulation to his knee, and worked out on the veterinary clinic's underwater treadmill."

"It's not a solution," said veterinarian Dr. Darryl Millis after the Cincinnati game. "It's a treatment. I anticipate at some point he will need surgery. We're treating him just as you would any other athlete and hoping for the best." That led to period of rehab when Smokey IX was not able to lead the team through the "T" and being otherwise "limited" on the sidelines. Eventually, Smokey IX ended up having ACL surgery on his right hind leg on January 24, 2012.

Earl Hudson said that Smokey's injury was an "aberration," that he couldn't remember anything similar, unless it were Smokey VIII eating the washcloth just before the BCS title game in Tempe against Florida State or Smokey VI having heat-related problems in 1991.

"The surgery went great," Dr. Millis said. "He is a really cooperative dog, inside and outside of surgery." The whole operation, focused on Smokey IX's right rear leg, took about 90 minutes, with Dr. Millis calling it "textbook." He also indicated the Smokey IX would have a similar operation in "4 to 6 weeks." Dr. Millis indicated that Smokey IX would be ready by the summer of

2012 and ready to get after North Carolina State in the season opener on September 1.

The line of Smokeys has always been ready for the season to start. When you think about it, that's been the byword for the Smokeys over the years.

Each one has come and gone, each making his own unique paw print on the University of Tennessee and those who have been involved with them. They've served well and faithfully.

EPILOGUE: FINAL THOUGHTS ON THE SMOKEYS AND A LOOK TO THE FUTURE

In the October 8, 1953, edition of the *Orange and White,* a student journalist named Shields Remine wrote prophetically about Smokey I making his debut two days later in the Vols' game against Chattanooga. The dog's debut was perceived to be something special, and Remine spared no words in detailing his hopes for the dog's future. Note also that he also got the dog's name correct, when other writers of that era couldn't seem to.

> For the first time in history, thanks to Mr. Worden and his Pep Club, we have a mascot—a very sad, all-knowing, sleepy hound dog named Smokey. We dig him the most. We hear reliably that Smokey is a barometer of Tennessee football fortunes, and he has been most morose these last two Saturdays. Perhaps with the invasion of the Moccasins, Smokey will let a smile split his dourness and the sun will again shine on the mighty Volunteers. On second thought, there are also elephants, tigers, wildcats, and admirals planning to invade these mole-ridden hills. With a bay and a bite we hope our dour friend will send them scurrying to their hideaways.

By the way, Smokey had a great deal to be happy about in that game against Chattanooga, since the Vols won 40–7. It certainly beat what had happened the previous two weeks, losses to Mississippi State and Duke by a combined total of 47–7.

Over the years, the Smokeys have grown on everybody involved, from the Brooks and Hudson families, to Stuart Worden, Harvey Sproul, and Remine, to the fans who have seen them in action. The dogs have truly led adventurous lives, as Dr. Klein has written.

In his eighth decade, Earl Hudson looks back over the now seven generations of Bluetick Coonhounds named Smokey, he does so with a great deal of pride and affection, perhaps even with a twinkle in his eye, now that he's the elder statesman in the history of the dogs and their relationship to the University of Tennessee. It's all about the nine dogs, of course, but, more importantly, it's about family. While Smokey and his image have changed with the times—sometimes controversially, as the recent trademark issue illustrates—the dog has been a dependable reminder of the importance of tradition at the university.

UT TRADEMARKS, SECONDARY MARKS, AND SMOKEY

There may have been a handshake deal between Bill Brooks and Stuart Worden when the deal was cut for Smokey I. But nearly sixty years later, the Smokey mascot, along with the entirety of the Vol athletic program, has become big business, with trademark, contractual, and licensing issues abounding, given the nature of today's society. The original Smokey trademark is registered by the state of Tennessee in 21 different Trademark and one Servicemark Classification.

For the record, the University of Tennessee holds State of Tennessee registration for the image of Smokey, dating to September 1, 1977, though the registration was not filed until 1981.

The usage of Smokey and his image is in line with a common law trademark. According to Mike Keener of UT's Office of Trademark Licensing, this means that "The university can prove ownership of the name."

The university's control of Smokey's image has not always been without controversy.

On April 13, 2005, U.T.'s Athletic Department unveiled six "secondary marks," enabling the university to integrate the tradition of Smokey into the logos and to "freshen up" some of its secondary marks or brands, according to a *Knoxville News Sentinel* story the next day. According to Chris Fuller, assistant athletics director in sales and marketing: "The primary brands for Tennessee athletics continue to be the 'Power T' and the 'Lady Vol T.' The 'Power T' and the 'Lady Vol T' from an overall standpoint are the right brands, but we felt something was missing. Our fans really identify with Smokey. These new secondary marks will give new energy to Smokey and add to the brand strength associated with our primary logos."

"A sports mark needs to have a little bit of aggressiveness to it without going over the top," said Knoxville illustrator Danny Wilson, who designed the new logo,

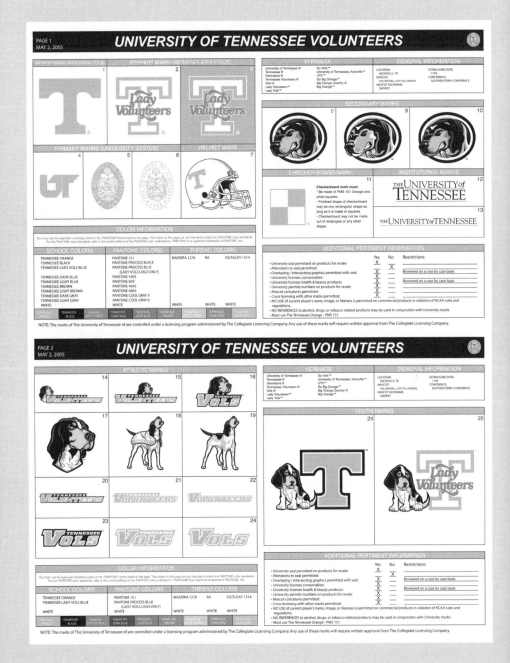

terming it the "Competitive Smokey." "You didn't want him foaming at the mouth or anything." There were also marks entitled "Youth Smokey" for Tennessee women's teams and "Dignified Smokey" for the men's teams.

"The new competitive version is a sleekly snarling menace of a hound clearly willing to mix it up with any of UT's opponents," Randy Kenner of the *News Sentinel* wrote.

The move to present a more aggressive-looking Smokey caused more than a few raised eyebrows among Vol fans, particularly the Hudsons, who have watched the rise of the mascot since the early days from the 1950s.

"New energy" was not among their comments about the so-called secondary marks.

"It's not in tune with the true spirit of Smokey," Earl Hudson argues. "I was disappointed in a way, but I understand their motives."

His wife, Bernice, was more blunt: "I don't like it."

That said, she added: "I don't think it's Smokey. Smokey's not aggressive like this dog looks."

What impact the merger of the university's men's and women's university athletic programs in the year 2012 and beyond will have on these logos and brandings is anybody's guess.

Bill and Mildred Brooks became a part of the history of the University of Tennessee and were part of the original story that started it all.

After Bill and Mildred died, Earl and Martha Hudson continued to take care of the dogs. Today, it's Earl, Bernice, and Earl's son Charles, the heir-apparent as caretaker of Smokey, continuing to loyally serve the Tennessee program. It's an impressive lineage and record of service by the respective families. "Bill was a proud owner of Smokey," Earl said of the development of the Bluetick mascot over the years. "He wanted to supply a dog that would excite the fans, give them a show of courage, and lead the team to be victorious." You couldn't help but think that Bill, were he around today, would be impressed with the way the line of dogs has progressed.

The dogs also had their impact on this year's handler. For his part, Moser offered this assessment of his interaction with Smokey IX. It's another example of the interaction between the dogs and those who have responsibility for

Earl and Martha at their home on Mountaincrest Drive with Smokey VIII. Earl Hudson collection.

them. "I remember having Smokey in my room," he said. "It felt like he was our dog, that I had 'bonded' with him."

As 2011 gave way to 2012, Earl Hudson talked about a changing of the guard. Smokey IX's future was in some doubt due to his knee injury, and Earl thinking about passing the torch to son Charles.

In October 2011, Moser was the first to hint that there might a change afoot where Smokey was concerned, paying tribute to what Earl had accomplished over the years.

"He's a great man," Moser said in October 2011, calling Earl Hudson "Mr. Earl" and Bernice "Miss Bernice." He termed Earl as "genuine," knowing as "much about Tennessee as anybody." Then he let out a secret. "I think 'Mr. Earl' is getting ready to hand it over to Charles. That's way above my head, but I wouldn't be surprised."

He was correct.

That actually did happen on November 10, 2011, when Charles picked up Smokey and took him to his home near Beaver Brook Country Club north of Knoxville. In what had to be an emotion-laden moment, the "changing of the guard" took place, albeit very quietly. Charles remembered that his dad called it a "momentous occasion," the passing of the dog from father to son.

"Charles has Smokey now. I retain ownership and am involved with him," Earl said. "I am not personally handling him. Charles does all the activities previously done by his father." Things were handled in a careful and positive manner, always thinking ahead, always thinking about what's best for the dog and the university, as is Earl's trademark. "We've already talked about a new dog. Smokey IX is eight years old. He'll be the mascot as long as he's viable."

When it becomes necessary to find Smokey X, he will "contact the United Kennel Club and request a letter on the bloodline." As he did when he found Smokey VIII and Smokey IX, "I'll tell them who I am and what I need."

Earl also said he looked forward to Charles taking responsibility for the dog. "Charles will do great. He's been a U.T. fan all these years. Smokey will

Smokey IX at Charles Hudson's house in March of 2012. Tom Mattingly.

adjust. He's over there now. They have a big, fenced-in yard. I'll still get to see him."

"Smokey's a smart dog," Charles said. "He's done well with the conversion. He gets along well with the neighbors." Charles also said that he had one specific wish. "I just hope to do as good a job as Uncle Bill and my dad did in being Smokey's owner."

But there's more, Earl said. "I'll miss him. We've been very close. He's a good dog to have around. He's a good protector." As all that talk was going on, Earl did have a confession to make about the dogs.

"Number 8 was my favorite," he said, "but number 9 is really coming on strong."

That's a great deal of attention for a dog, the cynics might say. Is it too much, too over the top? You be the judge.

How has the line of Smokeys affected Volunteer fans over the years? If you consider a letter written on the occasion of Smokey VIII's retirement by an obviously faithful Vol fan as an indicator, fans have taken the series of dogs as part of their "family," as one of their own.

Dear Smokey. We were looking through the paper the other day and came across an article written about you. With excitement, we began to read it. Sadly, we found out the article was about your recent diagnosis of cancer. Our hearts began to sadden. How could this be happening to the most important asset of the best college football team ever? To the one who for years and years goes out on the football field and braves the crowds, the weather, the wins and the losses, and loves every minute of it. Without you, the team would not be what they are. You are the pride of the Volunteers. Everyone loves you! I know there have been 7 Smokeys before you and there will be others after you, but in my eyes you are the only Smokey. I can remember taking my daughter to her first UT ball game, and she was so intrigued by you. She watched you the entire game. If she lost you, her little eyes searched and searched for you until she found you once again. You will always be with her, in her heart and memory. As long as our blood runs orange, you will always be a part of us. You are the heart and soul of the Volunteers. Great players come and go, but you, Smokey, are with us forever. Take your retirement and rest and be well. May God be with you and those who care for you. Cheers to the best bluetick coonhound and the greatest team that has ever graced a field. Thanks for the memories and GO BIG ORANGE! We hold our heads high for the University of Tennessee.

The mascot named Smokey, all nine of them now, is part of the tradition, part of the ambience of Tennessee football. Smokeys I through IX have been the top dogs on campus for more than fifty years.

There's only one Bluetick Coonhound in all of college football.

His name is Smokey.

This sign appears on the fence at Earl Hudson's home. Tom Mattingly.

NOTES

1. PROLOGUE

1. While quoted material in this book may refer to "blue tick coon hounds" or "bluetick coonhounds," the official name of the breed is "Bluetick Coonhound," as listed by the American Kennel Club. Outside of quotations, I'll use the official name or the shortened Bluetick.

2. "A long-standing tradition in our chapter is the training of the UT mascot, 'Smokey.' Since 1977, two of our brothers have been selected to care for the dog both on and off the playing field." Inter-Fraternity Council, University of Tennessee, Alpha, http://utkifc.com/agr. "UT Knoxville mascot Smokey has two AGRs as his handlers, a UT and AGR tradition since the '70s," Jim Nunn points out in "AGR Fraternity Celebrates its Impacts Across 60 Years," http://www.agriculture.utk.edu/publications/lls/Vol8No1spring/Vol8No1spring.pdf.

3. For the collection of programs, see http://diglib.lib.utk.edu/fbpro/main.php. The quotation is from a *Knoxville News Sentinel* article that can be found at http://www.knoxnews.com/news/2011/nov/01/artsclamation-items-range-10-to-5k/.

4. Over the years, Knoxville journalists have referred to the University of Tennessee as "U-T," "UT," and "U.T." The latter term seems to be in vogue currently and will be used in my text, apart from direct quotations.

5. Daniel's cartoons found in this book come from *You Are About to Experience One of the Most Thrilling Moments in Football When the Tennessee Volunteers Run Through the Big Tee . . . Pee* (Knoxville: Coleman Printing, 1983).

6. Ron Smith, *Every Saturday in Autumn: College Football's Greatest Traditions* (Sporting News, 2001), 28.

7. See Adriana Norton, "Do Mascots Increase School Spirit?" http://www.content4reprint.com/business/do-mascots-increase-school-spirit.htm.

8. Herbstreit quoted in Smith, *Every Saturday in Autumn,* 13

9. See "Fans earn college basketball's most beloved technical foul." http://rivals.yahoo.com/ncaa/basketball/blog/the_dagger/post/College-basketball-8217-s-best-technical-foul-r?urn=ncaab-wp5820.

10. See Lawrence Wells, *Football Powers of the South* (Oxford, Miss.: Yoknapatawpha Press, 1983); Barry Parker and Robin Hood, *Neyland: Life of a Stadium* (Chattanooga, Tenn.: Parker Hood Press, 2000); Tom Mattingly, *The University of Tennessee All-Access Football Vault* (Atlanta: Whitman Press, 2009). The two children's books are by Aimee Aryal: *Smokey's Journey through the Volunteer State* (Mascot Press, 2008) and *Hello, Smokey!* (Mascot Press, 2004).

11. Richard Ernsberger, Jr., *Bragging Rights: A Season Inside the SEC, College Football's Toughest Conference* (New York: M. Evans and Company, 2000), 342.

12. See The Sporting News, with a Foreword by Keith Jackson, *Saturday Shrines: College Football's Most Hallowed Grounds* (Sporting News, 2005), 155. Concerning the term Volunteers, the writers were right as far as they went. Here's an amplification from "Tennessee Traditions: Origins of Volunteers" at http://www.utsports.com/fans/traditions.html: "Tennessee acquired the name 'The Volunteer State' during the War of 1812. At the request of President James Madison, Gen. Andrew Jackson, who later became President himself, mustered 1,500 from his home state to fight at the Battle of New Orleans. The name became even more prominent in the Mexican War when Gov. Aaron Venable Brown issued a call for 2,800 men to battle Santa Ana and some 30,000 Tennesseans volunteered. Tennessee's color guard still wears dragoon uniforms of that era at all athletic events."

13. See Terry Shaw, "Bill Landry tells 'Heartland Series' stories in new book," http://www.knoxnews.com/news/2011/sep/10/bill-landry-tells-heartland-series-stories-in/.

14. See Tom Poste, "All About Smokey—The History of the Volunteers' Mascot," http://www.secsportsfan.com/all-about-smokey-the-history-of-the-volunteers-mascot.html.

2. LOOKING BACK

1. See "Spotlight Breed: The BlueTick Coonhound, http://members. petfinder.org/~MD149/Spotlightbluetick.html.

2. Tom Siler, *Tennessee's Dazzling Decade, 1960–1970* (Knoxville: Hubert E. Hodge Printing, 1970), 1.

3. See "The Top Mascots in College and Professional Sports," http:// www.usatoday.com/sports/2005-02-13-tenworstjobs-mascots-yarbrough_x. htm, February 13, 2005. Roy E. Yarbrough, Mascots: *The History of Senior College and University Mascots/Nicknames,* third edition (Bluff University Communications, 2004). For a convenient, if debatable, list of most famous mascots, see http://www.americasbestonline.net/cmascots.htm. Tennessee fans got well acquainted with Traveler when the Vols played at Southern Cal in 1981, and the horse ran the sidelines after every score in a 43–7 USC win. There were those from Tennessee in attendance who thought the barrage of USC points might bring the horse to its knees in exhaustion.

4. Milton M. Klein, *Volunteer Moments: Vignettes of the History of the University of Tennessee* (Knoxville: Univ. of Tennessee, 1996), 107.

5. Neal O'Steen, "The House That Neyland Built," University of Tennessee monograph (1980 insert to Georgia game program), xi. The card section was the subject of great discussion on campus and in campus media in 1953. An *Orange and White* editorial on November 5, 1953, had a harsh word for them, saying, in part, "They sometimes look rotten."

6. Bob Gilbert, *Neyland: The Gridiron General* (Savannah, Ga.,: Gold Coast, 1990), 199.

3. THE 1953 UNIVERSITY OF TENNESSEE CAMPUS SCENE

1. Betsey Beeler Creekmore, *Tennessee: A Celebration of 200 Years of the University* (Gibsonia, Pa.: Scripps Howard, 1994), 20.

2. This statement was made in a letter to Alfred Mynders, editor of the *Chattanooga Times.* See http://web.knoxnews.com/pdf/2011/jan/utholtletters.pdf.

3. Creekmore, *Tennessee*, 20.

4. Klein, *Volunteer Moments*, 70–71.

5. Ibid., 80.

4. THE TIDE OF TIMES IN TENNESSEE FOOTBALL, 1953

1. The phrase "tide of times" in this chapter title is from Roger Kahn, *The Boys of Summer* (New York: Harper and Row, 1972): "The Dodgers of 1953—not the pitching staff but the eight men in the field—can be put forth as the most gifted baseball team that has yet played in the tide of times" (p. 180).

2. Mattingly, *The University of Tennessee All-Access Football Vault*, 32–33.

3. Lindsey Nelson, *Hello, Everybody, I'm Lindsey Nelson* (New York: Beech Tree Books, 1985), 287.

4. Gilbert, *Neyland: The Gridiron General*, 210.

5. Siler, *Tennessee's Dazzling Decade*, 10–11.

6. This period produced seven All-America selections—Ted Daffer (twice), Horace (Bud) Sherrod, Hank Lauricella, Bill Pearman, John Michels, and Doug Atkins. There were also fourteen All-SEC selections, two Jacobs Trophy winners (for the SEC's best blocker), awarded to Jimmy Hahn and Michels, and a Heisman Trophy runner-up (Lauricella) over those three years. There were also four College Football Hall of Fame selections (Atkins, Lauricella, Michels, and General Neyland himself). It was a marvelous assemblage of talent.

7. Russ Bebb, *The Big Orange* (Huntsville, Ala.: Strode Publishing, 1973), 250.

8. These incidents are recalled in Ed Harris, *Golden Memories of Ed Harris: 50 Years in Big Orange Country* (1972), 20. Four days after the Vanderbilt contest would have been December 1, 1954. The dismissed staff were Ralph Chancey (who graduated in 1949), Johnson (who graduated in 1929), Al Hust (who graduated in 1943), Hodges "Burr" West (who graduated in 1941), Chan Caldwell (who graduated in 1948), and Bunzy O'Neil (who graduated in 1943). Also on staff were Emmett Lowery (a Purdue graduate, 1934), John Sines (Purdue, 1938), and John Idzik (Maryland, 1951).

9. Al Browning, *Tennessee vs. Alabama: Third Saturday in October, the Game-by-Game Story of the South's Most Intense Football Rivalry,* second edition (Nashville: Rutledge Hill, 2001), 136.

10. Robinson quoted by Harris, *Golden Memories,* 25.

11. Bebb, *The Big Orange,* 253.

12. Marvin West, *Legends of the Tennessee Vols* (Sports Publishing, 2005), 85. Note that in *Tales of the Tennessee Vols* (Sports Publishing, 2002), West makes mention of a "sportswriter" being pushed into the pool.

13. Quoted in Mattingly, *The University of Tennessee All-Access Football Vault,* 60.

5. THE BLUETICK COMETH

1. http://www.thepeoplehistory.com/1953.html. The hit songs for the year are listed at http://www.menziesera.com/number_1_hits/1953.shtml.

2. Peter Golenbock, *Dynasty: The New York Yankees, 1949–1964* (New York: Dover, 2010), 87.

3. In 1953, the *Knoxville Journal* was the city's morning newspaper, while the *Knoxville News-Sentinel,* as it was spelled then, published in the afternoon. Both newspapers had one Sunday edition. The *Journal* ceased Sunday publication in 1957. In 1986, the newspapers switched cycles, and the *News-Sentinel* became the morning paper. On December 31, 1991, the *Journal* ceased daily publication and became a weekly. In 2002, the *News-Sentinel* dropped the hyphen and became the *Knoxville News Sentinel.*

4. Johnny Majors, with Ben Byrd, *You Can Go Home Again* (Nashville: Rutledge Hill, 1986), 24.

5. Bebb, *The Big Orange,* 245.

6. The DyerGram was a staple of the *News Sentinel*'s coverage of Tennessee football from the October 5, 1935, North Carolina game, through the October 23, 1976, Florida game. "Dyer chronicled the games in pen and ink with a touch of whimsy thrown in for good measure," former Vol fullback and U.T. professor Andy Kozar has written. "Over the years, journalists have told the story of sports in a number of different ways. Bill Dyer did it with cartoons

interspersed between the play-by-play of the game." Tom Siler, *Tennessee: Football's Greatest Dynasty* (Knoxville: Holston Printing, 1862), 31.

7. Bob Phillips, "Going to College Gets a Coonhound a Better Job," *Prohound News Record: Coonhunting's Only Monthly News Report* (1983), pages not numbered.

6. THE LEGACY OF THE SMOKEYS

1. The *News Sentinel* also reported that day that Mayor-elect Jack Dance had named John Duncan, an assistant Knox County attorney general, as the city law director. For his part, Duncan would later become mayor and then be elected as a long-term member of Congress from the Knoxville area, where his son serves to this day.

2. "He Ain't Nothing But a Hound Dog, But, Oh What a Life Smokey Lives as UT's Mascot," *Tennessee Cooperator* (March 1988), Tennessee Farmer's Cooperative, La Vergne, Tenn., 1B. No author is given for this story.

3. See http://www.mmbolding.com/bowls/Sugar_1957.htm.

4. Klein, *Volunteer Moments*, 205.

5. Steve Fielder, "Tennessee's Blue tick Coonhound Mascot," *Coonhound Bloodlines* (May 1987), 86. There was to be an eerie parallel to a similar event involving Smokey IX in November 2011. "Smokey IX ate 6–8 chocolate coins," Bernice Hudson said. "We found the wrappers. We took him to the vet, and he was O.K."

6. Browning, *Tennessee vs. Alabama*, 223. Just to show how history occasionally gets confused, Marvin West reports this exchange took place before the 1970 game, on October 17, the day Tennessee intercepted eight passes against the Tide in a 24–0 Vol victory. Hunter was there for both games. Russ Bebb reports that it took place in 1968. A March 9, 2012, interview with Hunter confirmed that the "encounter," as he called it, did take place in 1968.

7. See Tom Poste's write-up on Smokey VI at http://www.secsportsfan. com/all-about-smokey-the-history-of-the-volunteers-mascot. html#ixzz1cNJgezC0.

8. Ibid.

9. See http://www.huffingtonpost.com/2010/02/16/sadie-the-scottish-terrie_n_464993.html.

10. For John Painter's utsports.com story, See http://www.utsports.com/sports/m-footbl/spec-rel/092911aao.html.

BOOKS BY THOMAS J. MATTINGLY

Tennessee Football: The Peyton Manning Years.
*The University of Tennessee Football Vault: The History of the Tennessee
      Volunteers*
The Tennessee Trivia Book
The University of Tennessee All-Access Football Vault

INDEX

Adams, John, 100

Agnes Scott University mascot "Scottie," 19

Aryal, Aimee (*Hello, Smokey*), 112n10

Aryal, Aimee (*Smokey's Journey through the Volunteer State*), 112n10

Ali Kahn pekense [sic], 82

Aloha Oe, 22

Alpha Gamma Rho (AGR) fraternity, 2, 6, 7, 26, 91, 111n2

Alumni Gymnasium, 54

American Broadcasting Company (ABC), 89

American Kennel Club, 99

Ames Brothers (*You, You, You*), 53

Anderson, Tom, 70

Andes, Julian, 54

Andy Holt Tower, 38

Animal Planet *Dogs*, 101 13, 20

Arrow Golden Oxford Shirts, 30

Assignment U-T, and Curt Mathis, 87

Associated Press, 34, 42, 61, 89, 100

Astro-Bluebonnet Bowl, Houston, 58, 92

Athens, Georgia, 9

Atlanta, Georgia, 21, 46

Auburn University, 5; "War Eagle," 5, 13

Austin High School, Knoxville, Tennessee, 33

Bailes, Red, 85

Baker, U.S. Representative Howard H., Sr., 44

Barbish, Bill (Moose), 64

Barker, Ruth Ann, 25, 69, 78

Battle, Bill, 22, 74, 75

Baylor Bear, 4, 116n3

Beach, Gladys, 24

Beaver Brook Country Club, 108

Bebb, Russ, 46, 49; (The Bluetick Cometh), 114n7, 115n11, 115n5

Big Orange Country, 14, 18, 74, 91

Big Orange Illustrated, 99

Big Sky Conference, 47

Bill's Clutch Shop, 50, 52, 81

Birmingham, Alabama, 22

Blair, Charles Edgar, 33

Blue Smoky, 60

Bluetick Coonhound, 1, 2, 4, 10, 14, 17, 19, 20, 21, 68, 73, 82, 89, 104, 110, 111n1, 113n1

Boling, Dr. Edward J., 31

Boston University mascot "Rhett," 19

Boyd, Bill, 21

Bozeman, Leon, 81

Brehm, Dr. C. E., 23, 26, 32, 54

Brogan, Beauchamp, 83, 84, 85, 86

Brooks, Mildred Hudson, 20, 21, 60, 65, 69, 73, 84, 86, 87, 94, 95; (The Legacy of the Smokeys), 116n2

Brooks, Rev. Willie Carson ("Bill," "Willie"), 6, 14, 18, 20, 21, 26, 50, 52, 61, 66, 67, 68, 73, 79, 80, 81, 82, 83, 86, 88, 94, 104, 106, 109

Brooks' Blue Smokey, 19, 20, 52, 58, 59, 64, 66, 69, 84

Brown v. Board of Education, 32, 34

Brown, Faye, 68

Browning, Al, 115n9, 116n6

Brownsville, Tennessee, 6

Broyles, Frank, 89

Bryant, Paul W. (Bear), 14, 49, 75, 89, 90, 91

Bullard M. M., 57

Burton, Jimmy, 82

Byerley's Cafeteria, 28, 29, 31

Byrd, Ben (*The Basketball Vols*), 34, 115n4

Byrd, Ben, 70

Callaway, Edna, 56

Camel Cigarettes ,30

Carolyn P. Brown Memorial Student Center, 10, 27, 47

Carousel Theatre, 29, 31

Cartersville, Georgia, 64

Chaplin, Charley, 53

Chattanooga, Tennessee, 67

Chase, Tommy, 95

Circle Park, University of Tennessee, 7

Civil War, 4

Clarksville, Tennessee, 7

Clement, Gov. Frank, 44

Clemson University, 96

Cleveland, Ohio, 64

Cleveland, Tennessee, 48, 64

College Football Hall of Fame, 31, 48

Como, Perry (*No Other Love, Don't Let the Stars Get in Your Eyes*), 53, 115n1

Coonhound, 38

Coonhound Bloodlines, 88

Corbin, Kentucky, 84

Cotton Bowl (1953), 43

Cowart, Betty, 72

Cracker Barrel restaurants, 10

Crawford, Denver, 61

Creager, Mickey, 60, 85

Creekmore, Betsey Beeler, 29, 32, 113n1; (*Looking Back*), 114n3

Cumberland Avenue, Knoxville, Tennessee, 30

D. C. Moody, 3

Daniel, Charles: (*UT Football Cartoons by Daniel, with Some Free Thoughts by Ben Byrd*), 4, 5, 88, 90, 111n4; (*You are About to Experience One of the Most Thrilling Moments in Football When the Tennessee Volunteers Run Through the Big Tee . . . Pee*), 111n5

Darning, Diane, 25, 69

Davis, Albert, 34, 36, 37

Delta Tau Delta fraternity, 83

Dennison, Sammy, 72

DeNovo, Dr. Robert, 95

Detroit Avenue, 22

Dickey, Doug, 11, 22, 34, 74, 88

Dodd, Bobby, 44, 82

Dogs of the SEC, 93

Dooley, Derek, 76

Dooley, Vince, 22

Dorothy Korby striped blouses, 30

Duke University, 25, 42, 69, 71, 103

Duncan, U.S. Rep. John J., Sr., 116n1

Dunford, Dr. Ralph D., 38

Dunn, Jimmy, 36

Duquesne University, 33, 34

Dye, Bill, 85

Dyer, Bill, 66, 115n6

DyerGram, 66

Eastabrook Hall, 54

Eisenhower, Brig. Gen. Dwight David, 22

Elam, Col. Tom, 46, 86

Ellis & Ernest Drug Store, 28, 29, 30

Ernest, Harold L., Jr., 14, 30, 56, 66

Ernest, Harold L., Sr., 30

Ernsberger, Dick, 14

Ernsberger, Richard, Jr. (*Bragging Rights: A Season Inside the SEC, College Football's Toughest Conference*), 14, 112n11

ESPN, 5; Sports Center 64

Faith, Percy (*Song from Moulin Rouge*), 53

Farouk's collies, 82

Feathers, Beattie, 44

Fielder, Steve, 88, 91, 116n5

Fields, A. L. (Bud), 65

Fiesta Bowl (1988), 97

Finebaum, Paul, 100

Fisher, Bob, 64

Fisher, Eddie, 53

Florida Citrus Bowl, 58
Flowers, Richmond, 11
Ford, Bud, 58
Ford, Gary D., 12
Fort Wayne, Indiana, 64
Fountain City, Tennessee, 50
Foxx, Bob, 54, 63
Franklin, Mack, 61, 64
Fresno State costumed mascot "Time-
    out," 19
Fuller, Chris, 104
Fulmer, Phillip, 76

Gardner-Webb University mascots
    "Lulu" and "Mac T. Bulldog," 19
Gardner, Dona, 60
Gate City, Virginia, 22
Gator Bowl, 58
Gay Street, Knoxville, Tennessee, 31, 52
Georgetown University mascot "Jack," 19
Georgia Tech University, 46
Gilbert, Bob (*Neyland: The Gridiron
    General*), 23, 45, 113n6; (*The Tide of
    Time . . .*), 114n4
Gilbert, Jeannie, 75
Gillespie, Willie Mae, 33
Glendale, Ohio, 64
Golenbock, Peter, 53, 115n2
Gonzaga University mascot "Spike," 19
Goodgame, Reverend Gordon, 14, 81
Goose Creek, South Carolina, 97
Gordy, John, 62
Gore, Senator Albert, Sr., 44
Grant Field, 21, 58
Gray, Eugene Mitchell, 32
Great Smoky Mountains National Park,
    20
Green, Ike, 57
Griffith, Ralph, 70

Hall's, 30
Hannon, Kent, 92, 99
Hammerskjold, Dag, 53
Harb, Joe, 45
Harrington, Heather, 100

Harris, Ed, 46, 114n8, 115n10
Harris, Jessie L., 38
Haslam, Jim, 22
Haynes, Will, 80, 81
Heartland Series, WBIR, 14
Herbstreit, Kirk, 5, 112n8
Herman Hickman Reader, 31
Hesler, Lexemuel Ray, 37
Hickman, Herman, 31
Hitt, Dick, 48
Holloway, Condredge, 22, 34
Holt, Dr. Andrew D. (Andy), 32, 33, 38, 39;
    The University of Tennessee Cam-
    pus Scene, 113n2
Homecoming, 22
Hood, Robin, 12
Hoskins, Dr. James D., 38
Hubbard, Hal, 44
Hudson, Bernice, 17, 20, 106, 107, 116n5
Hudson, Charles, 106, 107, 108, 109
Hudson, Earl, 6, 7, 13, 14, 17, 20, 26, 41, 50,
    52, 59, 60, 65, 66, 73, 83, 84, 86, 88, 94,
    95, 96, 99, 101, 104, 106, 107, 109, 110
Hudson, Martha, 17, 20, 73, 107
Hudson, Y. C., 26, 69
Huffington Post, 100
Humboldt, Tennessee, 25, 61
Hunter, Justin, 100
Hunter, Scott, 89
Huntland, Tennessee, 61
Huster, Edwin, Sr., 54, 63
Hyde, Jerry, 64

Jackson, Gen. Andrew, 14
Jenkins, Dan, 34
Jenkins, Lily, 32
Johnson, City Tennessee, 48
Johnson, L. B. (Farmer), 45
Judge, the Baylor Bear, 87, 88

Kahn, Roger (*The Boys of Summer*), 114n1
Keener, Mike, 104
Kefauver, Senator Estes, 44
Kennedy, John F., 88
Kenner, Randy, 106

Kiffin, Lane, 76
Kiner, Steve, 11
Klein, Dr. Milton, 22, 24, 33, 37, 38, 88, 92, 103, 113n3, 114n4, 114n5, 116n4
Knox County Baptist Association, 50
Knoxville Journal, 4, 34, 46, 54, 61, 65, 67, 70, 79, 81, 84, 88, 93, 114n115
Knoxville News Sentinel, 2, 5, 18, 23, 30, 44, 54, 58, 59, 60, 61, 70, 73, 85, 100, 106, 111n3, 115n3
Knoxville Volunteer Rescue Squad, 20
Kozar, Andy, 43, 115n6

Landry, Bill, 14
Leachman, Lamar, 64
Lee, Trygve, 53
Lenoir City, Tennessee, 28
Liberty Bowl Memorial Stadium, 3
L'il Abner, 25, 69
Lincoln Park, 81
Long, Neal, Jr., 21
Los Angeles Memorial Coliseum, 58
Los Angeles Times, 38
Louisiana State University, 24, 42
Louisiana State University mascot "Mike the Tiger," 14, 18
Louisville and Nashville Railroad West Knoxville Station, 30
Lower Second Creek Valley, 27,
Lucky Strike cigarettes, 30
Lynch, Heather, 11
Lynchburg, Tennessee, 62

Madisonville, Tennessee, 61
Majors, John, 61, 62, 74, 75, 76, 94, 115n4
Manning, Gus, 71
Mantle, Mickey, 30
Markelonis, Jo, 55
Market Street, Knoxville, Tennessee, 30
Martshall University, 76
Martin, Dr. Leslie, 86
Martin, Ray, 45
Mascot, Tennessee, 68, 72
Mascots, 18, 113n3

Mattingly, Tom, 7, 9, 12, 52, 79, 108, 112n10, 114n2, 115n13
Mauer, John, 33
McAdams, James Berlin (Trey), III, 6, 9
McClain, Lester, 34, 35, 36, 37
McCord, Darris, 64
McDonald, Jim, 74
McEver, Gene, 44
McGee, Costo, 20
McKeesport, Pennsylvania, 34
McManus, Gavin, 11
Mecca, 27
Memorial Coliseum, Lexington, Kentucky, 85, 86
Memphis Memorial Stadium, 30
Memphis State-Tennessee game (1969), 36
Metzler, Art, 63
Michie Stadium, West Point, New York, 75
Middlesboro, Kentucky, 84
Milan, Tennessee, 37
Miller's Department Store, 30
Millis, Dr. Darryl, 100, 101
Mink, Ray, 81
Mississippi State University, 3, 25, 41, 61, 64, 68, 81, 95, 103
Moody, D.C., 3
Mooney, George, 54, 63
Moore, Barbara J., 24
Moser, Robert, 7, 8, 106
Mountaincrest Drive, Knoxville, Tennessee, 6, 17, 107
Mt. Pleasant, Tennessee, 64

Nashville Banner, 49
Nanney, Becky, 91
Nelson, Lindsey ("*Hello, Everybody, I'm Lindsey Nelson*"), 44, 63; (The Tides of Time . . .), 114n3
New York Yankees, 30
Newport, Tennessee, 5
Neyland, Brig. Gen. Robert R., 10, 14, 22, 23, 41, 42, 43, 45, 46, 55, 56, 61, 88, 89, 114n6
Neyland: Life of a Stadium, 12, 112n10

Neyland Stadium, 1, 2, 27, 30, 31, 75, 76
North Carolina State University, 102
Northeastern University mascot "King
    Husky," 19
Northington, Nat, 34
Norton, Adriana, 4, 111n7

O'Steen, Neal, 22, 113n5
Oklahoma State University, 19
Ol' Rusty, 86
Old Smokey II, 85
On Top of Old Smoky, 86
Orange Nation, 10
Oschner Clinic, New Orleans, 88
Oswego, Kansas, 3

Page, Greg, 34
Page, Patti (*The Doggie in the Window*), 53
Painter, John, 117n10
Panama, 41
Parker, Barry, 12
Parker, Jackie, 64, 65
Paul Dean's Toggery, 30
Peach Bowl, 96, 97
Petfinder.org, 17
Phelps, Charley, 94
Phillips, Bob, 116n7
Pi Kappa Alpha fraternity, 24
Pierce, Chambliss, 58, 68
Pittman, Brad, 65, 67, 68
Pittsburgh, Pennsylvania, 34
Playboy magazine, 93
Poste, Tom, 15; (*All About Smokey—The
    History of the Volunteers' Mascot*),
    112n14
Postell-Gee, Joy, 21
Powell, John, 64
Presley, Elvis, 88
Price, Vincent, 53
Pritchard, Wes, 25, 69
*Prohound News Record: Coonhunting's
    Only Monthly Report*, 116n7
Prugh, Jeff, 38

Queen Elizabeth II, 52

Regas Restaurant, 31
Remine, Shields, 78, 103
Reynolds, Jack "Hacksaw," 11
Rice, Grantland, 44
Richardson, Keith, 75
Robinson, Harvey, 41, 44, 45, 46, 64, 73
Robinson, Theotis, Jr., 33
Rockne, Knute, 43
Rogersville, Tennessee, 20
Rose Avenue, 22
Rose Hole, 60, 61, 66
Rotroff, Roger, 64
Roy v. Brittain, 33
Russell, Fred, 49
Rutledge Pike, Knoxville, Tennessee
    ("Bloody 11W"), 6, 50, 68, 79, 81

Samford University mascot "Spike," 19
Sandusky, Ohio, 64
Schwanger, Ted, 64
Scott, Bob, 64
Scott, Bobby, 36
Seiler, Sonny, 92, 99
Shaw, Terry, 112n13
Shields-Watkins Field 1, 2, 4, 20, 21, 22,
    27, 28, 31, 34, 41, 57, 61, 64, 66, 67, 68,
    74, 81
Shelton, Betty, 68
Shula, Mike, 98
Sigma Phi Epsilon fraternity, 81
Siler, Tom, 18, 23, 30, 45, 73; (Look-
    ing Back), 113n2; (The Tide of
    Times . . .), 114n5; (The Bluetick
    Cometh), 116n7
Simon and Schuster, 31
Sloan, Steve, 48
Smith, Dora, 68
Smith, Ron (*Every Saturday in Autumn:
    College Football Greatest Traditions*),
    4, 111n6
Smokey (generic), 2, 4, 5, 9, 14, 15, 17, 19,
    22, 26, 57, 66, 73, 104, 105, 110

Smokey I (PR Brooks Blue Smokey), 18, 20, 24, 25, 65, 67, 68, 69, 70, 71, 78, 79, 81, 82, 103

Smokey II (PR Brooks' Blue Smokey II), 4, 21, 34, 74, 81, 82, 84, 85, 86, 87, 88, 89

Smokey III (PR Brooks' Blue Smokey III), 11, 58, 89, 91

Smokey IV (PR Brooks' Blue Smokey Joe), 74, 91, 92

Smokey V (PR Brooks' Blue Smokey V), 92, 93, 94

Smokey VI (PR Brooks' Blue Smokey VI), 65, 75, 94, 95

Smokey VII (PR Hudson's Blue Smokey VII), 76, 95, 116n7, 116n8

Smokey VIII (PR Hudson's Blue Smokey VIII), 11, 12, 76, 77, 92, 96, 97, 98, 109

Smokey IX (PR Hudson's Blue Smokey IX), 6, 7, 8, 10, 11, 12, 13, 14, 17, 20, 21, 76, 78, 97, 98, 99, 100, 107, 108, 109

Smokey's Howl, 10

Smokey's Palace, 10

Smokey's Tale, 10

Smoky (1950s name), 19, 20, 21, 25, 67, 70, 71, 78, 80, 81, 82

Smoky Mountains, 5

South Seventeenth Street, 29

Southeastern Conference (SEC), 13, 14, 48

Southern Clutch Shop, 52

Southern Living magazine (November 2005), 8, 12

Southern Living magazine (October 2006), 12

Southwestern Conference, 47

Sporting News Saturday Shrines: College Football's Most Hallowed Grounds, The, 14, 112n12

Sports Illustrated, 10

Sports Illustrated, September 23, 1968, 34

Sproul, Harvey, 14, 28, 78, 103

Spurrier, Steve, 48

Stadium Drive, Knoxville, Tennessee, 27

State of Tennessee General Assembly, 37

State of Tennessee song "Rocky Top," 10

Stenske, Dr. Kate, 97

Sterling House, 30

Stokely Athletics Center, 30

Stoll Field, Lexington, Kentucky, 86, 88

Streater, Jimmy, 34

Sugar Bowl, 58; 1957, 87, 88

Sun Bowl, 58

Sweetwater, Tennessee, 49

T-Room, 29

Tampa Stadium, 57

Tennessean, The, (Nashville's morning newspaper), 32

Tennessee Alumnus, 57

Tennessee Mill & Mine Supply Company, 41

Tennessee State University, 37

Tennessee Traditions: Origins of Volunteers, 111n12

Tennessee Walking Horse, 38, 57, 58

Texas A&M University Aggies, 13

Thayer, Harry (Hobo), 44

Thomas, Mary Lee, 68

Thompson, Ann, 68

Three Dog Night, 94

Tiger Walk (Auburn University), 10

Torch Night, 22

Tracy, Tom, 44

Traughber, Bill, 99

Tulane University, 30

Unitas, Johnny, 46

United Kennel Club, 108

United States, 4

United States Supreme Court, 32

University of Alabama Crimson Tide, 1, 13, 42, 45, 74, 75, 90, 91, 98, 99

University of Arkansas, 47, 89

University of California Los Angeles (UCLA), 94

University of Chattanooga, 42, 78, 103

University of Cincinnati, 100

University of Florida, 42, 46, 61, 89

University of Georgia Bulldogs, 9, 34; Russ, 99; Uga, 14, 34, 92, 96

University of Houston, 42, 67

University of Kentucky, 21, 42, 46, 61, 83

University of Louisville, 42, 76

University of Michigan Wolverines, 4

University of Mississippi (Ole Miss) Rebels, 14, 30

University of Missouri Tigers, 13

University of Nevada Las Vegas (UNLV), 97

University of Southern California mascot "Traveler," 19

University of Tennessee

—1953 Football Media Guide, 23, 45

—2010 Football Media Guide, 19

—2011 Football media Guide, 62

—All-Students Club, 54

—Athletic Department, 104

—Board of Trustees, 33

—College of Veterinary Medicine, 100

—*Daily Beacon,* 28

—Fraternity Row, 6

—"The Hill," 25, 27, 28, 31

—Independent students association, 80

—John C. Hodges Library, 31

—Library, 2; Special Collections, 29

—Office of Trademark Licensing, 104

—Oral History Project, 37

—*Orange and White* newspaper, 26, 28, 30, 53, 54, 63, 68, 69, 72, 78, 81, 82, 87, 103, 113n5

—Pep Club, 19, 24, 25, 26, 28, 50, 53, 57, 58, 60, 63, 68, 72, 81, 82, 84, 103

—Photographic Service, 28, 77

—"Power T," 104; "Lady Vol T," 104

—Pride of the Southland Marching Band, 1, 22

—school song: "Down the Field," 2; "Spirit of the Hill," 2

—Science Hall, 28, 29

—Sports Information Office, 35, 47, 48, 54, 62, 70, 98

—Veterinary Teaching Hospital, 95

—*Volunteer* yearbook, 82; 1953–54 24, 26, 30, 45; 1954–55, 25

University of Tennessee Football Vault, 12

University of Texas, 43

University of Texas mascot "Bevo," 19

University of Wyoming, 47

Updyke, Harvey, 100

USAToday.com, 19

Utsports.com, 100

Van Hoose, Alf, 49

Van Pelt, Shirley, 60

Vanderbilt University, 34, 42, 46, 86, 88

Vol Book Exchange, 30

Vol Network, 1, 54

Volopoly, 11

Volunteer Moments, 22, 37

Volunteer Navy, 10

Vowell, Morris, 46

Wade, Jimmy, 64

Walker, Scott, 97, 98

Wallace, Perry, 34

Ward, John ("Voice of the Vols"), 1, 54

Warmath, Murray, 44, 61, 64

WATE radio, 63

Waters, Dr. Eugene, 53

Weatherford, Jimmy, 91

Weaverville, North Carolina, 41

Wells, Lawrence (*Football Powers of the South*), 11, 112n10

West, Marvin (*Tales of the Tennessee Vols*), *41, 48, 115n12*

Westminster Kennel Club, 100

WETE radio, 63

Widoff, Wawanna Cameron, 14, 81

Williams, Al, 91

Williams, Jack, 11

Wilson, Bob, 71, 85

Wilson, Danny, 105

Wilson, Robert, 100

Woodruff, Bob, 36, 88, 96

Woody, 96

Woodruff, Joe, 89

Worden, Rechenbach & Brooke, 52

Worden, Stuart, 14, 24, 26, 50, 54, 55, 56, 57, 59, 60, 67, 68, 69, 72, 73, 74, 82, 103, 104

World War II, 28, 37, 41
WROL Radio, 63
WTBS Cable, 95
WTSK Television, 54
Wyatt, Bowden, 44, 46, 47, 48, 62, 74, 81, 88
Wyche, Bubba, 11, 34
Wynn, Herman D. (Breezy), 44

Yahoo! Sports 5, 112n9
Yale Avenue, 29; Urban Renewal Project, 31
Yale University mascot "Handsome Dan," 19
Young High School, Knoxville, Tennessee, 64